GIRLS
JUST WANNA
BAKE
Cupcakes

EASY, DELICIOUS DESSERTS
INSPIRED BY *the '80s*

Courtney Carey

CREATOR OF CAKE ME HOME TONIGHT

PAGE STREET
PUBLISHING CO.

PAGE STREET
PUBLISHING CO.

First published in 2024 by

Page Street Publishing Co.

27 Congress Street, Suite 1511

Salem, MA 01970

www.pagestreetpublishing.com

Distributed by Macmillan, sales in Canada by The Canadian Manda Group.

28 27 26 25 24   1 2 3 4 5

ISBN-13: 979-8-89003-028-3

Library of Congress Control Number: 2023944947

Edited by Krystle Green

Cover and book design by Rosie Stewart for Page Street Publishing Co.

Photography by Courtney Carey

Photography Assistance by James Pici

Author Headshots by Mark Duggan

Printed and bound in the United States of America

For my husband, Chris.
With your love and support, I can do anything I put my mind to.

For my girls, Carmen and Charlie.
You are the sweetest little things I've ever made.

Contents

CLASSIC DESSERTS TURNED UP TO 11 • 121

SWEET DREAMS ARE MADE OF THESE • 141

INTRODUCTION:
JUST CAN'T GET ENOUGH CUPCAKES

Greeting and salutations!

Who doesn't love a good dose of nostalgia? Adulting is hard. Bringing yourself back to the simplicities and fun of childhood is a great way to reconnect with your younger, less wrinkly self, whether you were an '80s baby like myself, or are an '80s baby at heart.

I started my baking blog, Cake Me Home Tonight, as a way to inspire new bakers and to help home bakers elevate their baking skills while having a little fun in the kitchen. As a self-taught home baker turned blogger, I have baked thousands upon thousands of cupcakes. Through many years of recipe development and taste testing (sorry, thighs), I have learned the art and science of cupcake baking and am thrilled to share my recipes with the world.

Baking cupcakes and all things '80s have always been my go-to stress relievers. There is just something about listening to '80s tunes that makes you want to dance, laugh and enjoy life. And you simply can't beat a good '80s flick. In my heart, and the hearts of many, the '80s are here to stay. And the same goes for cupcakes!

So, why are cupcakes totally rad? Cupcakes are for celebrating. They are perfectly portioned, portable, easy to make and so darn cute. Cupcakes are customizable and nostalgic, and we won't judge if you eat more than one. Every kid loves to pick a cupcake off a dessert table to lick off the frosting and give the cake to the nearest adult. Cupcakes can also feel less intimidating to bake than a decorated layer cake. The popularity of cupcakes has ebbed and flowed over the decades, but they always make an epic comeback, just like bodysuits and oversized blazers.

You will find a little something for everyone in this book. Each recipe will transport you back to some of the best childhood memories, whether it is opening your lunchbox and seeing your favorite treat or watching cartoons on the weekends with a big bowl of fruity cereal. My hope is that the recipes in this book will become instant classics and family favorites that you will bake over and over again. So, whether you need a delicious classic chocolate cupcake or something a little bit more extravagant with all the drizzles and sprinkles, I have you covered.

With each recipe, I've also included some of my favorite '80s tunes that you can crank up in your kitchen while making these delectable cupcakes. My mixtape, if you will. Through these songs and recipes, I hope to transport you to a time where mullets were considered a good idea, leg warmers kept our calves cozy and spandex was for all occasions. So, let's jump in our DeLorean, hit 88 miles per hour and blow out 16 candles on our birthday cupcakes.

Have a totally awesome time baking!

Courtney

BECOME A TOTALLY AWESOME CUPCAKE BAKING PRO

Baking cupcakes is a little art and a little weird science. But instead of designing our ideal woman, we are designing sweet little masterpieces! Baking from scratch can feel more intimidating than Rocky Balboa to Clubber Lang. But, if you have the basic skills and know a secret or two, you will be baking perfect, bakery-quality cupcakes to impress your friends and family like Maverick buzzing the tower.

In this section, we will cover the basics of baking and decorating cupcakes. I will let you in on some of my favorite tips for baking perfectly moist and fluffy cupcakes, as well as making smooth and creamy buttercream frosting. You will learn how to effortlessly fill a cupcake and pipe beautiful swirls of frosting to make your cupcakes look ace to the max. Whether you are a new cupcake baker or a cupcake wizard, knowing the basics is always totally righteous.

TEN TIPS FOR BAKING EPIC CUPCAKES

Baking the perfect cupcake is a breeze if you have the basics down. Like Mr. Miyagi reminds us, "First learn stand, then learn fly." Here are 10 simple tips and tricks to help you bake the best cupcakes and make the most of the recipes in this book.

1. Use Room Temperature Ingredients

Bring the chilled ingredients (butter, milk, sour cream, eggs) to room temperature before making the cupcake batter. This step is often overlooked, which can lead to problems with the texture of the cupcakes. When the ingredients are all at the same temperature, they play nice together and create an emulsion, which contributes to a moist and tender cupcake crumb.

2. Prioritize Quality Where It Counts

You don't need to buy the most expensive ingredients to make a delicious cupcake, but it is helpful to know where to prioritize quality. I recommend going with pure vanilla extract over imitation vanilla for the best flavor. Dark cocoa powder adds a deeper and richer chocolate flavor than regular cocoa. Use fresh lemon or lime zest and juice for a bright citrus flavor. Use baking powder and baking soda within six months of opening to keep them fresh and to help the cupcakes rise perfectly. If you notice your cupcakes aren't rising properly, you might want to purchase fresh baking powder and baking soda.

3. Do Not Undermix or Overmix

When creaming butter and sugar, we want the mixture to become light, pale and fluffy before adding additional wet or dry ingredients. Alternating the addition of the dry and wet ingredients ensures that the flour is properly hydrated and the batter isn't overmixed. Once the batter comes together and no dry ingredients remain, stop mixing. Overmixing the cupcake batter can lead to the development of gluten, which can create tough and chewy cupcakes.

4. Don't Forget to Scrape the Bowl

It is always a good idea to scrape the sides and bottom of the mixing bowl periodically when making the cupcake batter. This ensures that all the ingredients are well combined and there are no pockets of flour or chunks of butter that could create problems with taste and texture.

5. Use a Cookie Scoop

My favorite way to portion out cupcake batter is to use a large cookie scoop that holds about 3 tablespoons (45 ml) of batter. This is the perfect amount of batter to fill a standard cupcake liner and ensures that your cupcakes are uniform in size and bake evenly. If the recipe calls for the liner to be filled two-thirds full, you will need one large scoopful; if it is to be three-quarters full, you will need a heaping large scoopful.

6. Bake the Cupcakes on the Center Rack

Bake the cupcakes, one pan at a time, on the center rack of your oven for the perfect rise. If the cupcakes are too close to the top of the oven, the tops will brown and dry out. If the cupcakes are too close to the bottom of the oven, the bottoms can burn and the cupcakes may not rise properly.

7. Use the Touch Test

Many bakers like to use a toothpick to test their cupcakes, but I find that a touch test is a better way to determine whether the cupcakes are perfectly baked. When the timer rings, gently (and carefully) touch the top of the cupcakes. If the cake bounces back, the cupcakes are ready. If your fingertip leaves an indent, bake the cupcakes for an additional minute or two.

8. Remove the Cupcakes from the Pan to Cool

Did you know that cupcakes continue to bake even after you have removed the pan from the oven? Cooling the cupcakes in the pan can lead to overbaked and dry cupcakes. To prevent this, let the cupcakes cool in the pan for about 5 minutes and then carefully transfer them to a wire rack to cool to room temperature.

9. Let the Cupcakes Cool Completely

After baking, be sure to cool the cupcakes to room temperature before adding any filling or frosting. If the cupcakes are not properly cooled, they can easily crumble when coring and filling. Additionally, buttercream and whipped cream frosting will quickly melt on a warm cupcake.

10. Store the Cupcakes in an Airtight Container

The best way to store cupcakes to preserve their freshness is in an airtight container. I recommend purchasing a cupcake carrier container. Most buttercream cupcakes can be stored at room temperature for a day or two and in the refrigerator for three to five days. Cupcakes containing custard fillings, cream cheese frosting or whipped cream frosting should always be stored in the refrigerator. Buttercream cupcakes are best served at room temperature, so remove the cupcakes from the refrigerator an hour or two before serving. You can also freeze unfrosted cupcakes by individually wrapping the cupcakes in plastic wrap and storing them in a plastic ziplock freezer bag for up to one month.

TEN TIPS FOR MAKING BODACIOUS BUTTERCREAM FROSTING

Just like Doc Martens to leather and lace, frosting can make or break a cupcake. So, it's time to beat it and whip it good, and talk about 10 tips for making the best buttercream frosting.

1. Use Room Temperature Unsalted Butter

Bringing the butter to room temperature helps the butter whip up well and creates smooth and creamy frosting. If the butter is cold, it will be difficult to cream. You also don't want the butter to be too warm or too soft. The best way to check for the perfect butter consistency is to press your finger into the stick of butter. If it indents with some resistance and maintains its shape, you are ready to make the buttercream. To bring the butter to room temperature quickly, simply cut the butter into small pieces and it will be ready in no time. If the butter is too soft, chill it in the refrigerator for about 15 minutes to firm it up a bit before making the buttercream.

2. Paddle vs Whisk Attachment

Pay close attention to the instructions for the frosting recipes. For many of the buttercream recipes, I recommend using a paddle attachment to make a smooth and creamy buttercream. Some of the frosting recipes (e.g., Swiss meringue buttercream, whipped cream, ermine buttercream and cream cheese frosting) will instruct you to use a whisk attachment. For these frosting recipes, we want to incorporate air to make the frosting light and fluffy. If you do not have a stand mixer, don't fret! You can use an electric hand mixer to make the frosting recipes. It might take a little extra time and elbow grease, but the frosting will look and taste amazing.

3. Whip the Butter Before Adding the Powdered Sugar

This step is the key to creating a light and creamy buttercream frosting. Whip the butter for at least 5 minutes before adding any additional ingredients. This incorporates a little bit of air into the butter, making the butter light and pale in color. The finished buttercream will have a very smooth and creamy consistency.

4. Sift Lumpy Powdered Sugar

If there are lumps in your powdered sugar or it appears to be coarse, it is helpful to sift the powdered sugar before adding it to the butter. Test out different brands of powdered sugar to find your favorite. Some are finer than others, which can affect the texture of the buttercream. If there are no lumps, you can skip the sifting.

5. Don't Skip the Salt

Adding a pinch of salt to the buttercream frosting contrasts the sweetness and enhances the flavor of the frosting. Feel free to adjust the amount of salt in the frosting recipes in this book based on your own personal taste, but I don't recommend skipping the salt altogether, or using salted butter in buttercream recipes, so that you can control the amount of salt.

6. Heavy Cream Is Buttercream's Best Friend

Drizzling heavy cream into the buttercream helps create the smooth, rich, velvety texture of the frosting. The heavy cream helps dissolve some of the powdered sugar and brings everything together. You could substitute milk or half-and-half for the heavy cream, but the high fat content in the cream is a game changer.

7. Tint the Buttercream with Gel Food Coloring

Gel food coloring is the best for coloring buttercream. It is highly pigmented, so a little goes a long way and it does not change the taste or texture of the buttercream.

8. Scrape the Bowl Each Time You Add Ingredients

When making the buttercream, it is important to scrape the sides and bottom of the bowl occasionally to ensure that all the ingredients are well combined. I recommend scraping the bowl a few times when whipping the butter, after the addition of each ingredient and during the final whipping phase.

9. Smooth the Buttercream Before Piping

There are three tricks I like to use to remove air bubbles and smooth out the buttercream: You can stir the frosting by hand with a spatula for a few minutes to push out any air pockets. Another trick is to mix the buttercream on low speed with a paddle attachment for about 10 minutes. Or you could also melt about ¼ cup (60 ml) of the buttercream in a microwave for 10 seconds. While mixing on low speed with the paddle attachment, drizzle in the melted buttercream and watch as it magically becomes super creamy and smooth.

10. Make the Buttercream Frosting Ahead of Time

You can make the buttercream frosting up to a week ahead of time. Store the buttercream in an airtight container or wrapped in plastic wrap in the refrigerator. When you are ready to frost the cupcakes, bring the buttercream to room temperature and whip it for several minutes until it is as good as new. There are two exceptions to this rule: (1) Make whipped cream frosting the day you plan on icing the cupcakes, as it will not rewhip like buttercream; and (2) make buttercream that contains cookie bits the day you plan on frosting the cupcakes, as the cookie bits will dissolve if stored and rewhipped.

HOW TO FILL AND FROST CUPCAKES TO THE MAX

Now that we have our epic cupcakes and bodacious buttercream, we have to put them all together into totally awesome cupcakes. Let's talk about how to easily fill cupcakes and create the most rad frosting swirls to make your cupcakes look and taste amazing.

How to Fill the Cupcakes

The easiest and fastest way to fill cupcakes is to use an apple corer. If you do not have an apple corer on hand, you can also use a sharp paring knife to remove the center of the cupcakes.

1. Hold the apple corer vertically and push it into the center of the cupcake about two-thirds of the way down. Do not go all the way to the bottom of the cupcake.

2. Twist the apple corer and pull the corer out of the cupcake to remove the center cake.

3. Fill the center of the cupcake with filling using a piping bag.

How to Frost the Cupcakes

To pipe the frosting onto the cupcakes, you will need a piping bag and piping tips. An 18-inch (45-cm) piping bag will hold the exact amount of frosting you need to pipe one batch of cupcakes.

For the cupcakes pictured in this book, I used Wilton® 1A, 1M and 2D tips, and Ateco 826, 857 and 869 tips. In each recipe, I specify which tip to use to replicate the buttercream swirl style shown in the pictures.

Making Buttercream Swirls

Speaking of swirls, four different buttercream swirl styles are used in this book to create these fun and enticing cupcakes.

Rose Swirl >>

Start with the piping tip above the center of the cupcake. Without releasing the pressure, pipe a swirl that is tight around the center and continue to swirl outward until the top of the cupcake is covered. As you are completing the swirl, decrease the pressure on the piping bag and stop squeezing before pulling the piping tip away.

<< Double Swirl

Repeat the same steps as the rose swirl, starting in the center and swirling the frosting over the entire surface of the cupcake. Once you reach the edge of the cupcake, lift the piping tip to create a second layer of frosting along the edges of the cupcake. When you reach the end of the second layer, decrease the pressure on the piping bag and pull the piping tip away.

<< Ice Cream Swirl

Start with the piping tip above the center of the cupcake. Without releasing the pressure, pipe a swirl around the center to cover the top of the cupcake. As you continue to pipe, move the tip upward and inward as you swirl. End the swirl in the center of the cupcake. Stop squeezing and pull the tip upward. Pretend that you work at the local ice cream shop doling out soft-serve ice cream.

Ruffle Swirl >>

For the ruffle swirl, you will follow the same steps as the ice cream swirl, but with two small differences. First, as you are piping, gently wiggle the piping tip to create the swirl pattern. The other difference is that you will need to put a bit more pressure on the piping bag to make the frosting flow out a bit faster to create the ruffle. The best piping tip to use to create a ruffle swirl is the Wilton 2D piping tip.

THE BRAT
Pack

These days, we like to think of basic as boring, but back in the '80s, it was hip to be square. Sometimes the simplest flavors are the best! Whether you love bright and fruity flavors, rich and fudgy chocolate, or fun and colorful birthday cupcakes, there is always something there for everyone.

In this chapter, you will find some of my favorite classic cupcake recipes that take flavor to the next level. We are amping up vanilla cupcakes with extra flavor from vanilla bean paste (page 19). Why not add a bit of brown butter to cream cheese frosting for carrot cake cupcakes (page 31)? Need the perfect wedding cupcake? Well, as Billy Idol says, it's a nice day for a white wedding cupcake (page 35). My hope is that these recipes will become your go-to classic cupcake recipes that you will reach for over and over again. Feel free to get a little crazy and mix and match the cupcake and buttercream recipes. By mastering these classic cupcake flavors, you will be a cupcake baking hero in no time at all.

VALLEY GIRL VANILLA BEAN CUPCAKES

Where we're going we don't need roads, but we will need cupcakes. Might I suggest trying out this tasty take on a classic? They are packed with vanilla flavor from pure vanilla extract and vanilla bean paste, and the vanilla bean buttercream frosting might just save your life. If my calculations are correct, when your oven hits 350°F (177°C), you're going to see some serious deliciousness. These cupcakes are so tasty, they will have you shouting, "Great Scott!"

VANILLA BEAN CUPCAKES

1¼ cups (156 g) all-purpose flour

1½ tsp (7 g) baking powder

½ tsp salt

¾ cup (150 g) granulated sugar

¼ cup (57 g/½ stick) unsalted butter, at room temperature

¼ cup (60 ml) vegetable oil

1 large egg, at room temperature

2 tbsp (30 ml) sour cream, at room temperature

2 tsp (10 ml) vanilla extract

1 tsp vanilla bean paste

½ cup (120 ml) milk, at room temperature

VANILLA BEAN BUTTERCREAM FROSTING

1 cup (227 g/2 sticks) unsalted butter, at room temperature

2½ cups (300 g) powdered sugar

1 tsp vanilla extract

1 tsp vanilla bean paste

¼ tsp salt

2 tbsp (30 ml) heavy cream

ADDITIONAL INGREDIENTS

1 tbsp (15 g) colorful nonpareil sprinkles

VANILLA BEAN CUPCAKES

Preheat the oven to 350°F (177°C). Line a cupcake pan with 12 cupcake liners.

In a medium-sized bowl, whisk together the flour, baking powder and salt. Set aside.

In a large bowl, use an electric mixer to cream together the granulated sugar, butter and vegetable oil until pale and creamy. Add the egg, sour cream, vanilla extract and vanilla bean paste. Mix on medium speed until well combined. Add half of the flour mixture and mix on low speed until incorporated. Slowly pour in the milk while mixing on low speed. Add the remaining half of the flour mixture and mix until combined and smooth.

Portion the cupcake batter into the cupcake liners about three-quarters full. Bake the cupcakes for 20 minutes, or until they bounce back when gently touched. Remove them from the oven and let the cupcakes cool in the pan for 5 minutes, then transfer to a wire rack to cool completely.

VANILLA BEAN BUTTERCREAM FROSTING

In the bowl of a stand mixer fitted with a paddle attachment, whip the butter on medium-high speed for 5 minutes, or until pale and creamy. Add the powdered sugar and mix on low speed until fully incorporated with the butter. Add the vanilla extract, vanilla bean paste and salt. Slowly drizzle in the heavy cream until fully incorporated. Scrape the sides and bottom of the bowl as needed. Turn the mixer to medium speed and whip the buttercream for 2 to 3 minutes, or until light and creamy.

ASSEMBLING THE CUPCAKES

Fill a piping bag fitted with a Wilton 1M piping tip with the vanilla bean buttercream frosting. Pipe an "ice cream swirl" (see page 15 for more instructions) of buttercream on the cupcakes and sprinkle with colorful nonpareil sprinkles.

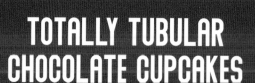

TOTALLY TUBULAR CHOCOLATE CUPCAKES

SONG: Wang Chung—Everybody Have Fun Tonight (1986)

YIELD: 12 cupcakes

I'll drive a million miles to eat chocolate cupcakes tonight. So, if you're feeling low, turn up your oven. These cupcakes are moist and have a rich and fudgy chocolate flavor. Adding a swirl of chocolate buttercream frosting puts them over the top. So, rip it up and don't forget to let them cool down before frosting, because you need this cupcake and she needs you.

CHOCOLATE CUPCAKES

¾ cup (180 ml) boiling water

¼ cup (42 g) semisweet or dark chocolate chips

¼ cup (25 g) dark cocoa powder

1 tsp instant espresso powder

¾ cup (94 g) all-purpose flour

¾ cup (150 g) granulated sugar

½ tsp baking soda

½ tsp salt

⅓ cup (80 ml) vegetable oil

2 large eggs, at room temperature

1 tsp vanilla extract

CHOCOLATE BUTTERCREAM FROSTING

1 cup (227 g/2 sticks) unsalted butter, at room temperature

2½ cups (300 g) powdered sugar

⅓ cup (33 g) dark cocoa powder

1 tsp vanilla extract

¼ tsp salt

2 tbsp (30 ml) heavy cream

ADDITIONAL INGREDIENTS

2 tbsp (30 g) rainbow sprinkles

CHOCOLATE CUPCAKES

Preheat the oven to 350°F (177°C). Line a cupcake pan with 12 cupcake liners.

In a medium-sized bowl, stir together the boiling water, chocolate chips, dark cocoa powder and instant espresso powder until the chocolate chips are melted. Set the chocolate mixture aside to cool for 5 minutes.

In a large bowl, whisk together the flour, granulated sugar, baking soda and salt. Pour the cooled chocolate mixture into the flour mixture and whisk until well combined. Add the vegetable oil, eggs and vanilla, and whisk until the batter is smooth.

Pour the cupcake batter into the cupcake liners about two-thirds full. Bake the cupcakes for 20 minutes, or until they spring back when gently touched. Remove them from the oven and let the cupcakes cool in the pan for 5 minutes, then transfer to a wire rack to cool completely.

CHOCOLATE BUTTERCREAM FROSTING

In the bowl of a stand mixer fitted with a paddle attachment, whip the butter on medium-high speed for 5 minutes, or until pale and creamy. Add the powdered sugar and dark cocoa powder and mix on low speed until fully incorporated. Add the vanilla and salt. While mixing on low speed, slowly drizzle in the heavy cream. Scrape the sides and bottom of the bowl as needed. Turn the mixer to medium speed and whip the buttercream for 2 to 3 minutes, or until smooth and creamy.

ASSEMBLING THE CUPCAKES

Fill a piping bag fitted with an Ateco 826 piping tip with the chocolate buttercream frosting. Pipe an "ice cream swirl" (see page 15 for more instructions) of chocolate buttercream onto the cupcakes. For a pop of color, add colorful rainbow sprinkles to the cupcakes.

SONG: Madonna—Holiday (1983)

YIELD: 12 cupcakes

COWABUNGA CONFETTI CUPCAKES

Everybody spread the word, we're going to have a cupcake celebration! Is it possible to say no to a confetti cupcake? There is nothing like one to bring back all of those happy days. These cupcakes have amazing vanilla almond flavor and are packed with colorful rainbow sprinkles. The creamy vanilla buttercream frosting will make you forget about the bad times. If we could have an endless supply of these confetti cupcakes, it would be, it would be so nice.

CONFETTI CUPCAKES

1¼ cups (156 g) all-purpose flour

1½ tsp (7 g) baking powder

½ tsp salt

¾ cup (150 g) granulated sugar

¼ cup (57 g/½ stick) unsalted butter, at room temperature

¼ cup (60 ml) vegetable oil

2 large egg whites, at room temperature

2 tbsp (30 ml) sour cream, at room temperature

1½ tsp (8 ml) vanilla extract

½ tsp almond extract

½ cup (120 ml) milk, at room temperature

¼ cup (45 g) rainbow sprinkles

VANILLA BUTTERCREAM FROSTING

1 cup (227 g/2 sticks) unsalted butter, at room temperature

2½ cups (300 g) powdered sugar

2 tsp (10 ml) vanilla extract

¼ tsp salt

2 tbsp (30 ml) heavy cream

2 to 3 drops sky blue gel food coloring

ADDITIONAL INGREDIENTS

2 tbsp (30 g) rainbow sprinkles

CONFETTI CUPCAKES

Preheat the oven to 350°F (177°C). Prepare a cupcake pan with 12 cupcake liners.

In a medium-sized bowl, whisk together the flour, baking powder and salt. Set aside.

In a large bowl, use an electric mixer to cream together the granulated sugar, butter and vegetable oil until light, pale and creamy. Add the egg whites, sour cream, vanilla and almond extract. Mix on medium speed until smooth. Add half of the flour mixture and mix on low speed until mostly combined. Slowly pour in the milk while continuing to mix on low speed. Add the remaining half of the flour mixture and mix until combined and smooth. Fold in the rainbow sprinkles.

Portion the cupcake batter into the cupcake liners about three-quarters full. Bake the cupcakes for 20 minutes, or until they bounce back when gently touched. Remove them from the oven and let the cupcakes cool in the pan for 5 minutes, then transfer to a wire rack to cool completely.

VANILLA BUTTERCREAM FROSTING

In the bowl of a stand mixer fitted with a paddle attachment, whip the butter on medium-high speed for 5 minutes, or until pale and creamy. Add the powdered sugar and mix on low speed until fully incorporated with the butter. Add the vanilla and salt. Slowly drizzle in the heavy cream and add a few drops of gel food coloring. Scrape the sides and bottom of the bowl as needed. Turn the mixer to medium speed and whip the buttercream for 2 to 3 minutes, or until smooth and creamy.

ASSEMBLING THE CUPCAKES

Fill a piping bag fitted with an Ateco 826 piping tip with the vanilla buttercream frosting. Pipe an "ice cream swirl" (see page 15 for more instructions) of buttercream onto the confetti cupcakes. Decorate the cupcakes with colorful rainbow sprinkles.

RADICAL RED VELVET CUPCAKES

SONG: Nena—99 Red Balloons (1983)

YIELD: 12 cupcakes

This is the recipe we've waited for. These red velvet cupcakes are moist and tender, and flavored with a bit of cocoa powder and buttermilk. They are more red than a D.A.R.E. t-shirt and *The Shining* put together. The perfect complement to the cake is a swirl of sweet and tangy cream cheese frosting. You will end up eating the whole dozen, until one by one, they are gone. So, better make 99 red velvet cupcakes!

RED VELVET CUPCAKES

1¼ cups (156 g) all-purpose flour

1 tbsp (5 g) unsweetened cocoa powder

¾ tsp baking soda

½ tsp salt

¾ cup (150 g) granulated sugar

½ cup (120 ml) vegetable oil

1 large egg, at room temperature

2 tsp (10 ml) vanilla extract

½ tsp white vinegar

1 tsp red gel food coloring

½ cup (120 ml) buttermilk, at room temperature

CREAM CHEESE FROSTING

¾ cup (170 g/1½ sticks) unsalted butter, at room temperature

4 oz (113 g) cream cheese, at room temperature

2½ cups (300 g) powdered sugar

2 tsp (10 ml) vanilla extract

¼ tsp salt

ADDITIONAL INGREDIENTS

1 tbsp (15 g) red and white sprinkles

RED VELVET CUPCAKES

Preheat the oven to 350°F (177°C). Line a cupcake pan with 12 cupcake liners.

In a medium-sized bowl, whisk together the flour, cocoa powder, baking soda and salt. Set aside.

In a large bowl, use an electric mixer to mix the granulated sugar, vegetable oil, egg, vanilla, vinegar and red gel food coloring until well combined. Add half of the flour mixture to the red mixture and mix on low speed until well incorporated. Slowly pour in the buttermilk while mixing on low speed, and then add the remaining half of the flour mixture and mix until the red velvet batter is smooth.

Portion the cupcake batter into the cupcake liners about three-quarters full. Bake the cupcakes for 20 minutes, or until they spring back when gently touched. Remove them from the oven and let the cupcakes cool in the pan for 5 minutes, then transfer to a wire rack to cool to room temperature.

CREAM CHEESE FROSTING

In the bowl of a stand mixer fitted with a whisk attachment, whip the butter and cream cheese on medium-high speed until light, fluffy and smooth. Add the powdered sugar, vanilla and salt. Mix on low speed until all the ingredients are well combined. Scrape the sides and bottom of the bowl as needed. Turn the mixer to medium-high speed and whip the frosting for an additional 2 to 3 minutes until light and fluffy.

ASSEMBLING THE CUPCAKES

Fill a piping bag fitted with an Ateco 826 piping tip with the cream cheese frosting. Pipe an "ice cream swirl" (see page 15 for more instructions) of frosting onto the red velvet cupcakes and sprinkle with red and white sprinkles.

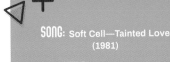
LEGIT LEMON CUPCAKES

Sometimes I feel I've got to, dun dun, eat a cupcake. Say hello and wave good-bye to these delicious cupcakes that are flavored with fresh lemon juice and zest for bright citrus flavor and swirled with a tangy lemon buttercream frosting. Sweet like Duckie and sour like Steff, these cupcakes will knock your socks off.

LEMON CUPCAKES

1¼ cups (156 g) all-purpose flour

1½ tsp (7 g) baking powder

½ tsp salt

¾ cup (150 g) granulated sugar

¼ cup (57 g/½ stick) unsalted butter, at room temperature

¼ cup (60 ml) vegetable oil

1 large egg, at room temperature

2 tbsp (30 ml) sour cream, at room temperature

1 tsp lemon zest

¼ cup (60 ml) fresh lemon juice

¼ cup (60 ml) milk, at room temperature

LEMON BUTTERCREAM FROSTING

1 cup (227 g/2 sticks) unsalted butter, at room temperature

2½ cups (300 g) powdered sugar

1 tsp lemon zest

¼ tsp salt

2 tbsp (30 ml) fresh lemon juice

1 tbsp (15 ml) heavy cream

ADDITIONAL INGREDIENTS

12 lemon slices

LEMON CUPCAKES

Preheat the oven to 350°F (177°C). Line a cupcake pan with 12 cupcake liners.

In a medium-sized bowl, whisk together the flour, baking powder and salt. Set aside.

In a large bowl, use an electric mixer to cream together the granulated sugar, butter and vegetable oil until light, pale and smooth. Add the egg, sour cream and lemon zest, and mix on medium speed until well combined. Add half of the flour mixture and mix on low speed until incorporated. Slowly pour in the lemon juice and milk while mixing on low speed, and then add the remaining half of the flour mixture and mix until combined and smooth.

Portion the cupcake batter into the cupcake liners about three-quarters full. Bake the cupcakes for 20 minutes, or until they bounce back when gently touched. Remove them from the oven and let the cupcakes cool in the pan for 5 minutes, then transfer to a wire rack to cool completely.

LEMON BUTTERCREAM FROSTING

In the bowl of a stand mixer fitted with a paddle attachment, whip the butter on medium-high speed for 5 minutes, or until pale and creamy. Add the powdered sugar and mix on low speed until fully incorporated with the butter. Add the lemon zest and salt. Slowly drizzle in the lemon juice and heavy cream until fully incorporated. Scrape the sides and bottom of the bowl as needed. Turn the mixer to medium speed and whip the buttercream for 2 to 3 minutes, or until smooth and creamy.

ASSEMBLING THE CUPCAKES

Fill a piping bag fitted with a Wilton 1M piping tip with the lemon buttercream frosting. Pipe a "double swirl" (see page 13 for more instructions) of lemon buttercream onto the lemon cupcakes and add a slice of lemon to the top of each cupcake.

BIG TIME BIRTHDAY CUPCAKES

SONG: Kool & The Gang—Celebration (1980)

YIELD: 12 cupcakes

Celebrate good times with cupcakes! There's a party going on right here, and we are bringing the fun and the dessert. These birthday cupcakes are the classic combination of yellow cake with a creamy chocolate buttercream frosting. Adding a ton of rainbow sprinkles and 16 candles will put these treats over the top. So, what's your pleasure? Totally these cupcakes!

YELLOW CUPCAKES

1¼ cups (156 g) all-purpose flour

1½ tsp (7 g) baking powder

½ tsp salt

¾ cup (150 g) granulated sugar

¼ cup (57 g/½ stick) unsalted butter, at room temperature

¼ cup (60 ml) vegetable oil

1 large egg, at room temperature

2 large egg yolks, at room temperature

1 tbsp (15 ml) sour cream, at room temperature

2 tsp (10 ml) vanilla extract

½ cup (120 ml) milk, at room temperature

CHOCOLATE BUTTERCREAM FROSTING

1 cup (168 g) dark chocolate chips

1 cup (227 g/2 sticks) unsalted butter, at room temperature

2 cups (240 g) powdered sugar

1 tsp vanilla extract

¼ tsp salt

2 tbsp (30 ml) heavy cream

ADDITIONAL INGREDIENTS

2 tbsp (30 g) rainbow sprinkles

YELLOW CUPCAKES

Preheat the oven to 350°F (177°C). Prepare a cupcake pan with 12 cupcake liners.

In a medium-sized bowl, whisk together the flour, baking powder and salt. Set aside.

In a large bowl, cream together the granulated sugar, butter and vegetable oil with an electric mixer until light, pale and smooth. Add the egg, egg yolks, sour cream and vanilla. Mix on medium speed until smooth. Add half of the flour mixture and mix on low speed until mostly combined. Slowly pour in the milk while mixing on low speed and then add the remaining half of the flour mixture and mix until the batter is smooth.

Portion the cupcake batter into the cupcake liners about three-quarters full. Bake the cupcakes for 20 minutes, or until they spring back when gently touched. Remove them from the oven and let the cupcakes cool in the pan for 5 minutes, then transfer to a wire rack to cool to room temperature.

CHOCOLATE BUTTERCREAM FROSTING

In a microwave-safe bowl, microwave the dark chocolate chips for 30 seconds, then stir. Heat the chocolate for another 15 seconds and stir. Repeat this process until the chocolate is melted and smooth. Set aside to cool for 5 to 10 minutes.

In the bowl of a stand mixer fitted with a paddle attachment, whip the butter on medium-high speed for 5 minutes, or until pale and creamy. Add the cooled melted chocolate and mix to combine. Add the powdered sugar, vanilla and salt. Mix on low speed until smooth. Drizzle in the heavy cream. Scrape the bowl to ensure the ingredients are well combined. Turn the mixer to medium speed and whip the buttercream for 2 to 3 minutes, or until smooth and creamy.

ASSEMBLING THE CUPCAKES

Fill a piping bag fitted with a Wilton 2D piping tip with the chocolate buttercream frosting. Pipe a "ruffle swirl" (see page 15 for more instructions) of the buttercream on the cupcakes and sprinkle with rainbow sprinkles, because it is time to blow out the candles and celebrate.

KILLER CARROT CAKE CUPCAKES

Oh, I hear the music, close my eyes, bake the cupcakes. These will take hold of your heart. They have the warm carrot cake flavors of vanilla and cinnamon, and the brown butter cream cheese frosting adds a nutty, caramelized flavor. So, grab your leg warmers and prepare to dance as you whip up these delicious treats. Side bonus: Dancing will help burn off extra calories, so have as many cupcakes as your heart desires.

CARROT CUPCAKES

1¼ cups (156 g) all-purpose flour

1½ tsp (7 g) baking powder

1½ tsp (5 g) ground cinnamon

½ tsp salt

⅛ tsp baking soda

¾ cup (150 g) granulated sugar

¼ cup (57 g/½ stick) unsalted butter, at room temperature

¼ cup (60 ml) vegetable oil

1 large egg, at room temperature

1 tbsp (15 ml) sour cream, at room temperature

2 tsp (10 ml) vanilla extract

1 cup (110 g) finely grated carrot

⅓ cup (80 ml) buttermilk, at room temperature

BROWN BUTTER CREAM CHEESE FROSTING

¾ cup (170 g/1½ sticks) unsalted butter

4 oz (113 g) cream cheese, at room temperature

2½ cups (300 g) powdered sugar

2 tsp (10 ml) vanilla extract

¼ tsp salt

ADDITIONAL INGREDIENTS

1 tbsp (15 g) orange sprinkles

CARROT CUPCAKES

Preheat the oven to 350°F (177°C). Line a cupcake pan with 12 cupcake liners.

In a medium-sized bowl, whisk together the flour, baking powder, cinnamon, salt and baking soda. Set aside.

In a large bowl, cream together the granulated sugar, butter and vegetable oil with an electric mixer until smooth. Add the egg, sour cream and vanilla, and mix until creamy. Stir in the grated carrot. Add half of the flour mixture and mix on low speed. Slowly pour in the buttermilk, continuing to mix on low speed, and then add the remaining half of the flour mixture and mix until the batter is well incorporated.

Portion the cupcake batter into the cupcake liners about three-quarters full. Bake the cupcakes for 20 minutes, or until their tops bounce back when gently touched. Remove them from the oven and let the cupcakes cool in the pan for 5 minutes, then transfer to a wire cooling rack.

BROWN BUTTER CREAM CHEESE FROSTING

In a small saucepan, melt and cook the butter over medium-low heat, stirring occasionally, until light golden-brown. Immediately pour the browned butter into a heatproof bowl, let it cool to room temperature and then chill until the butter solidifies. Bring the brown butter to room temperature before making the frosting.

In the bowl of a stand mixer fitted with a whisk attachment, whip the softened brown butter and cream cheese on medium-high speed until smooth and creamy. Add the powdered sugar, vanilla and salt, and mix on low speed until combined. Turn the mixer to medium speed and whip the frosting for an additional 2 to 3 minutes until smooth and creamy.

ASSEMBLING THE CUPCAKES

Fill a piping bag fitted with an Ateco 869 piping tip with the brown butter cream cheese frosting. Pipe a "rose swirl" (see page 13 for more instructions) of frosting onto the carrot cupcakes. Decorate the cupcakes with orange sprinkles.

STELLAR STRAWBERRY CUPCAKES

SONG: Belinda Carlisle—Heaven Is a Place on Earth (1987)

YIELD: 12 cupcakes

After you bake these cupcakes, heaven will be a place in your kitchen. If you are mad about strawberries, they will make you dance and put you in a trance. The fresh strawberry flavor comes from strawberry reduction, which is concentrated, puréed strawberries. Strawberry Shortcake and the Berrykins would be totally impressed with your berrylicious baking skills. When I feel alone, I reach for these cupcakes. Don't feel guilty for eating more than one because my lips are sealed.

STRAWBERRY CUPCAKES

1¼ cups (156 g) all-purpose flour

1½ tsp (7 g) baking powder

½ tsp salt

⅛ tsp baking soda

¾ cup (150 g) granulated sugar

¼ cup (57 g/½ stick) unsalted butter, at room temperature

¼ cup (60 ml) vegetable oil

2 large egg whites, at room temperature

2 tsp (10 ml) vanilla extract

½ cup (120 ml) strawberry Berrylicious Berry Reduction (page 151)

¼ cup (60 ml) buttermilk, at room temperature

Drop of pink gel food coloring

STRAWBERRY BUTTERCREAM FROSTING

1 cup (227 g/2 sticks) unsalted butter, at room temperature

2½ cups (300 g) powdered sugar

¼ cup (60 ml) strawberry Berrylicious Berry Reduction (page 151)

1 tsp vanilla extract

¼ tsp salt

1 tbsp (15 ml) heavy cream

ADDITIONAL INGREDIENTS

1 tbsp (15 g) pastel nonpareil sprinkles

6 small strawberries, halved

STRAWBERRY CUPCAKES

Preheat the oven to 350°F (177°C). Line a cupcake pan with 12 cupcake liners.

In a medium-sized bowl, whisk together the flour, baking powder, salt and baking soda. Set aside.

In a large bowl, use an electric mixer to cream together the granulated sugar, butter and vegetable oil until pale and smooth. Add the egg whites and vanilla, and mix on medium speed until well combined. Add half of the flour mixture to the batter and mix on low speed until incorporated. Pour in the strawberry reduction, buttermilk and pink gel food coloring, and mix on low speed. Add the remaining half of the flour mixture and mix until the batter is smooth.

Portion the cupcake batter into the cupcake liners about three-quarters full. Bake the cupcakes for 20 minutes, or until their tops spring back when touched. Remove them from the oven and let the cupcakes cool in the pan for 5 minutes, then transfer to a wire rack to cool completely.

STRAWBERRY BUTTERCREAM FROSTING

In the bowl of a stand mixer fitted with a paddle attachment, whip the butter on medium-high speed for 5 minutes, or until pale and creamy. Add the powdered sugar and mix on low speed until fully incorporated with the butter. Add the strawberry reduction, vanilla and salt. Slowly drizzle in the heavy cream until fully incorporated. Scrape the sides and bottom of the bowl as needed. Turn the mixer to medium speed and whip the buttercream for 5 to 10 minutes, or until smooth and creamy.

ASSEMBLING THE CUPCAKES

Fill a piping bag fitted with a Wilton 1M piping tip with the strawberry buttercream frosting. Pipe an "ice cream swirl" (see page 15 for more instructions) of the buttercream onto the strawberry cupcakes. Decorate the cupcakes with pastel nonpareil sprinkles and fresh strawberries.

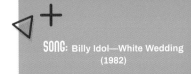

SONG: Billy Idol—White Wedding (1982)

YIELD: 12 cupcakes

IT'S A NICE DAY FOR WHITE WEDDING CUPCAKES

It's a nice day to bake some white wedding cupcakes. If you want all the fun of an '80s wedding without the big hair, blue eyeshadow and puffy sleeves, you must try this recipe. The white almond cupcakes are moist and as fluffy as an '80s wedding dress. And they are swirled with a meringue buttercream frosting that is smoother than any wedding singer. What's my vice and wish? These cupcakes. Now that we've had the cake, time to party on, dudes!

WHITE ALMOND CUPCAKES

1¼ cups (156 g) all-purpose flour

1½ tsp (7 g) baking powder

½ tsp salt

¾ cup (150 g) granulated sugar

¼ cup (57 g/½ stick) unsalted butter, at room temperature

¼ cup (60 ml) vegetable oil

2 large egg whites, at room temperature

2 tbsp (30 ml) sour cream, at room temperature

1 tsp almond extract

1 tsp vanilla extract

½ cup (120 ml) milk, at room temperature

MERINGUE BUTTERCREAM FROSTING

3 oz (90 ml) pasteurized egg whites (from a carton), at room temperature

2½ cups (300 g) powdered sugar

1 tsp almond extract

1 tsp vanilla extract

¼ tsp salt

1 cup (227 g/2 sticks) unsalted butter, at room temperature

ADDITIONAL INGREDIENTS

1 tbsp (15 g) silver dragee sprinkles

Silver luster dust

WHITE ALMOND CUPCAKES

Preheat the oven to 350°F (177°C). Line a cupcake pan with 12 cupcake liners.

In a medium-sized bowl, whisk together the flour, baking powder and salt. Set aside.

In a large bowl, cream together the granulated sugar, butter and vegetable oil with an electric mixer until pale and smooth. Add the egg whites, sour cream, almond extract and vanilla, and mix on medium speed until well combined. Add half of the flour mixture and mix on low speed until incorporated. Slowly pour in the milk while mixing on low speed. Add the remaining half of the flour mixture and mix until the cupcake batter is smooth.

Portion the cupcake batter into the cupcake liners about three-quarters full. Bake the cupcakes for 20 minutes, or until their tops spring back when gently touched. Remove them from the oven and let the cupcakes cool in the pan for 5 minutes, then transfer to a wire rack to cool to room temperature.

MERINGUE BUTTERCREAM FROSTING

In the bowl of a stand mixer fitted with a whisk attachment, whip the egg whites and powdered sugar on medium-high speed for 5 to 10 minutes, or until the mixture is thick and opaque. Add the almond extract, vanilla and salt. Turn the mixer to low speed and add the softened butter, 1 tablespoon (14 g) at a time, mixing in between each addition. Turn the mixer to medium-high speed and whip, scraping the bowl occasionally, for 10 to 15 minutes, or until the frosting is smooth and creamy.

ASSEMBLING THE CUPCAKES

Fill a piping bag fitted with a Wilton 2D piping tip with the meringue buttercream. Pipe a "ruffle swirl" (see page 15 for more instructions) of buttercream onto the cooled cupcakes. Sprinkle with silver dragee sprinkles and silver luster dust, and let's get hitched!

PRETTY IN PINK CHERRY CUPCAKES

SONG: The Psychedelic Furs—
Pretty in Pink (1981)

YIELD: 12 cupcakes

This cupcake is pretty in pink, isn't she? These little beauties are made with maraschino cherries. The cherry buttercream frosting is light and fluffy, just like Andie's prom dress. Don't waste good lip gloss when you get the frosting all over your face. My best friend's sister's boyfriend's brother's girlfriend heard from this guy who knows this kid who's going with the girl who said these are, like, the best cherry cupcakes ever.

CHERRY CUPCAKES

1¼ cups (156 g) all-purpose flour

1½ tsp (7 g) baking powder

½ tsp salt

¾ cup (150 g) granulated sugar

¼ cup (57 g/½ stick) unsalted butter, at room temperature

¼ cup (60 ml) vegetable oil

2 large egg whites, at room temperature

2 tbsp (30 ml) sour cream, at room temperature

1 tsp vanilla extract

6 tbsp (90 ml) milk, at room temperature

2 tbsp (30 ml) maraschino cherry juice

½ cup (110 g) chopped maraschino cherries

CHERRY BUTTERCREAM FROSTING

1 cup (227 g/2 sticks) unsalted butter, at room temperature

2½ cups (300 g) powdered sugar

1 tsp vanilla extract

¼ tsp salt

3 tbsp (45 ml) maraschino cherry juice

2 tbsp (30 ml) heavy cream

ADDITIONAL INGREDIENTS

12 maraschino cherries

1 tbsp (15 g) pink sprinkles

CHERRY CUPCAKES

Preheat the oven to 350°F (177°C). Line a cupcake pan with 12 cupcake liners.

In a medium-sized bowl, whisk together the flour, baking powder and salt. Set aside.

In a large bowl, use an electric mixer to cream together the granulated sugar, butter and vegetable oil until creamy. Add the egg whites, sour cream and vanilla, and mix on medium speed until smooth. Add half of the flour mixture and mix on low speed until incorporated. Slowly pour in the milk and maraschino cherry juice, continuing to mix on low speed. Add the remaining half of the flour mixture and mix until the batter is smooth. Fold in the chopped maraschino cherries.

Portion the cupcake batter into the cupcake liners about three-quarters full. Bake the cupcakes for 20 minutes, or until their tops bounce back when gently touched. Remove them from the oven and let the cupcakes cool in the pan for 5 minutes, then transfer to a wire rack to cool completely.

CHERRY BUTTERCREAM FROSTING

In the bowl of a stand mixer fitted with a paddle attachment, cream the butter on medium-high speed for 5 minutes, or until pale and creamy. Add the powdered sugar and mix on low speed until fully incorporated with the butter. Add the vanilla and salt. Slowly drizzle in the maraschino cherry juice and heavy cream, mixing until fully incorporated. Scrape the sides and bottom of the bowl as needed. Turn the mixer to medium speed and whip the buttercream for 2 to 3 minutes, or until smooth and creamy.

ASSEMBLING THE CUPCAKES

Fill a piping bag fitted with a Wilton 1M piping tip with the cherry buttercream. Pipe an "ice cream swirl" (see page 15 for more instructions) of the frosting onto the cupcakes. Add a maraschino cherry and pink sprinkles to each cupcake and let's head off to the prom!

DON'T YOU FORGET ABOUT
These Treats

Picture this. You sit down at the cafeteria table with your Cabbage Patch Kids lunchbox. You slowly open the lid, fearful of the potential horrors that await you. Will you find a bologna sandwich? Carrot sticks? Box of raisins? Suddenly, all your fears and doubts rush away as you see an individually wrapped, stunningly swirled Hostess® cupcake staring back at you. Now, all is right in the world and it's going to be the best day ever. And, no, Tiffany, I will not trade you for your fruit cup!

The cupcake recipes in this chapter are inspired by some of our favorite lunchbox treats, nostalgic cafeteria sweets and Saturday morning breakfast memories. Let's turn PB & J's and fluffernutter sandwiches into dessert (pages 49 and 58), make dreamsicles and strawberry crunch bars unmeltable (pages 54 and 41) and create cupcakes inspired by our favorite breakfast foods so we can easily rationalize eating cupcakes in the morning. I hope these flavors bring you back to fond childhood memories with your favorite group of friends. Were you more like the Goonies, the Lost Boys, the Heathers or the Breakfast Club?

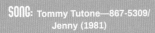
STUNNING STRAWBERRY CRUNCH CUPCAKES

For a good time, make these cupcakes. I think we can all agree that strawberry crunch ice cream bars reigned supreme in the school cafeteria. These fresh strawberry cupcakes are topped with ermine buttercream to give them a creamy, dreamy vanilla ice cream flavor. Of course, we are piling on homemade strawberry crunch because more is always better. How many would you like? I want 8,675,309.

STRAWBERRY CUPCAKES

1¼ cups (156 g) all-purpose flour

1½ tsp (7 g) baking powder

½ tsp salt

⅛ tsp baking soda

¾ cup (150 g) granulated sugar

¼ cup (57 g/½ stick) unsalted butter, at room temperature

¼ cup (60 ml) vegetable oil

2 large egg whites, at room temperature

2 tsp (10 ml) vanilla extract

½ cup (120 ml) strawberry Berrylicious Berry Reduction (page 151)

¼ cup (60 ml) buttermilk, at room temperature

Drop of pink gel food coloring

ERMINE BUTTERCREAM FROSTING

1 cup (200 g) granulated sugar

1 cup (240 ml) milk

⅓ cup (41 g) all-purpose flour

1 cup (227 g/2 sticks) unsalted butter, at room temperature

1 tsp vanilla extract

¼ tsp salt

STRAWBERRY CRUNCH

10 vanilla sandwich cookies, crushed

2 tbsp (28 g) unsalted butter, melted

1½ tbsp (22 g) strawberry gelatin powder

ADDITIONAL INGREDIENTS

6 small strawberries, halved

STRAWBERRY CUPCAKES

Preheat the oven to 350°F (177°C). Line a cupcake pan with 12 cupcake liners. In a medium-sized bowl, whisk together the flour, baking powder, salt and baking soda. Set aside.

In a large bowl, use an electric mixer to cream together the granulated sugar, butter and vegetable oil until creamy. Add the egg whites and vanilla, and mix until well combined. Add half of the flour mixture and mix on low speed. Pour in the strawberry reduction, buttermilk and pink gel food coloring, while continuing to mix. Add the remaining half of the flour mixture and mix until the batter is smooth.

Portion the cupcake batter into the cupcake liners about three-quarters full. Bake the cupcakes for 20 minutes, or until they spring back when touched. Remove them from the oven and let the cupcakes cool in the pan for 5 minutes, then transfer to a wire rack to cool completely.

ERMINE BUTTERCREAM FROSTING

In a medium-sized saucepan over medium-low heat, whisk together the granulated sugar, milk and flour. Cook the mixture, stirring frequently, for 10 minutes, or until it has a thick, custard-like consistency. Cool the custard to room temperature and then chill for 1 hour before making the buttercream.

In the bowl of a stand mixer fitted with a whisk attachment, whip the butter for 5 minutes, or until creamy. While mixing on low speed, slowly spoon in the cooled custard mixture. Add the vanilla and salt. Increase the speed to medium-high and whip, scraping the bowl occasionally, for 10 to 12 minutes, or until the buttercream has the consistency of whipped cream.

STRAWBERRY CRUNCH

In a small bowl, stir together the vanilla sandwich cookie crumbs, melted butter and strawberry gelatin powder.

ASSEMBLING THE CUPCAKES

Fill a piping bag fitted with a Wilton 1A piping tip with half of the ermine buttercream. Pipe a "rose swirl" (see page 13 for more instructions) of frosting onto the cupcakes. Press the frosting into the strawberry crunch. Fill a piping bag fitted with a Wilton 1M piping tip with the remaining buttercream. Pipe a small swirl of buttercream onto the cupcakes, sprinkle with the remaining strawberry crunch and decorate with halved strawberries.

SNAP, CRACKLE, POP CRISPY RICE TREATS CUPCAKES

SONG: Naked Eyes—Always Something There to Remind Me (1982)

YIELD: 12 cupcakes

How excited were you to open your Care Bears lunchbox and see Rice Krispies Treats®? There is always something there to remind me about how clutch these sticky, sweet treats are. These cupcakes are made with tender vanilla cake and marshmallow buttercream frosting, topped with a classic crispy rice treat. If you are in the mood for some snap, crackle and pop, these cupcakes will put a smile on your face and totally count as breakfast, right?

VANILLA CUPCAKES

1¼ cups (156 g) all-purpose flour

1½ tsp (7 g) baking powder

½ tsp salt

¾ cup (150 g) granulated sugar

¼ cup (57 g/½ stick) unsalted butter, at room temperature

¼ cup (60 ml) vegetable oil

1 large egg, at room temperature

2 tbsp (30 ml) sour cream, at room temperature

2 tsp (10 ml) vanilla extract

½ cup (120 ml) milk, at room temperature

MARSHMALLOW BUTTERCREAM FROSTING

1 cup (227 g/2 sticks) unsalted butter, at room temperature

2 cups (200 g) marshmallow fluff

1½ cups (180 g) powdered sugar

2 tsp (10 ml) vanilla extract

¼ tsp salt

2 tbsp (30 ml) heavy cream

CRISPY RICE TREATS

2 tbsp (28 g) unsalted butter

5 oz (142 g) mini marshmallows (approximately 2½ cups)

½ tsp vanilla extract

2½ cups (67 g) crispy rice cereal (I prefer Rice Krispies brand)

1 tbsp (15 g) rainbow sprinkles

ADDITIONAL INGREDIENTS

1 tbsp (15 g) rainbow nonpareil sprinkles

VANILLA CUPCAKES

Preheat the oven to 350°F (177°C). Line a cupcake pan with 12 cupcake liners.

In a medium-sized bowl, whisk together the flour, baking powder and salt. Set aside.

In a large bowl, use an electric mixer to cream together the granulated sugar, butter and vegetable oil until smooth. Add the egg, sour cream and vanilla, and mix on medium speed until well combined. Add half of the flour mixture to the batter and mix on low speed. Slowly pour in the milk and then add the remaining half of the flour mixture. Mix until the batter is smooth.

Portion the cupcake batter into the cupcake liners about three-quarters full. Bake the cupcakes for 20 minutes, or until they bounce back when touched. Remove them from the oven and let the cupcakes cool in the pan for 5 minutes, then transfer to a wire rack to cool completely.

MARSHMALLOW BUTTERCREAM FROSTING

In the bowl of a stand mixer fitted with a paddle attachment, whip the butter on medium-high speed for 5 minutes, or until pale and creamy. Add the marshmallow fluff and mix until smooth. Add the powdered sugar, vanilla, salt and heavy cream, and mix on low speed until fully incorporated. Turn the mixer to medium speed and whip the buttercream for 2 to 3 minutes, or until smooth and creamy.

CRISPY RICE TREATS

In a medium-sized saucepan over low heat, stir together the butter, mini marshmallows and vanilla until melted and smooth. Pour the crispy rice cereal into the marshmallow mixture and stir to coat. Fold in the rainbow sprinkles. Divide the mixture into 12 equal parts and, using moist hands, roll the treats into spheres.

ASSEMBLING THE CUPCAKES

Fill a piping bag fitted with an Ateco 869 piping tip with the marshmallow buttercream frosting. Pipe a "rose swirl" (see page 13 for more instructions) of buttercream onto the cupcakes, sprinkle with the rainbow nonpareil sprinkles and top each cupcake with a crispy rice treat.

SPACE AGE BROWNIE CUPCAKES

Surely you've heard of Cosmic Brownies. I have, and don't call me Shirley. These copycat Cosmic Brownies cupcakes are out of this world. E.T. would phone home to tell everyone how rad they are. Made with fudgy, chewy brownie cake, they are iced with chocolate fudge frosting and studded with rainbow chip candies for that classic star-studded look. You will have to use "the Schwartz" to stop yourself from noshing on the whole batch. You will be falling in love with this recipe.

BROWNIE CUPCAKES

1 cup (125 g) all-purpose flour

⅔ cup (66 g) dark cocoa powder

½ tsp baking powder

½ tsp salt

1 cup (220 g) packed light brown sugar

¾ cup (170 g/1½ sticks) unsalted butter, cubed

½ cup (100 g) granulated sugar

2 large eggs, at room temperature

¼ cup (60 ml) vegetable oil

1 tsp vanilla extract

CHOCOLATE FUDGE FROSTING

1½ cups (250 g) semisweet chocolate chips

1 cup (120 g) powdered sugar

¾ cup (180 ml) heavy cream

½ cup (114 g/1 stick) unsalted butter

1 tsp vanilla extract

¼ tsp salt

ADDITIONAL INGREDIENTS

2 tbsp (35 g) rainbow chip candies

BROWNIE CUPCAKES

Preheat the oven to 350°F (177°C). Line two cupcake pans with 12 or 13 cupcake liners.

In a medium-sized bowl, whisk together the flour, dark cocoa powder, baking powder and salt. Set aside.

In a microwave-safe bowl, combine the light brown sugar and butter. Heat in a microwave for 90 seconds, or until the butter is melted. Stir until the butter and brown sugar are well combined and smooth. Set aside.

In a separate large bowl, use an electric mixer to whip the granulated sugar and eggs until the mixture is light and pale. Slowly drizzle in the brown sugar mixture while mixing on low speed to temper the egg mixture. Add the vegetable oil and vanilla, and mix well. Pour the flour mixture into the egg mixture and mix on low speed until the batter is smooth.

Portion the brownie batter into the cupcake liners about three-quarters full. Bake the cupcakes for about 24 minutes, or until their tops are set. Remove them from the oven and let the cupcakes cool in the pans for 5 minutes, then transfer to a wire rack to cool completely.

CHOCOLATE FUDGE FROSTING

In a medium-sized saucepan, combine the chocolate chips, powdered sugar, heavy cream, butter, vanilla and salt. Place the saucepan over medium-low heat and stir occasionally until the mixture is smooth. Transfer the frosting to a bowl and let it cool to room temperature. Then, cover and chill in the refrigerator for an hour or two until thickened, stirring the mixture occasionally while chilling to prevent lumps from forming. The frosting is ready when it has the consistency of peanut butter.

ASSEMBLING THE CUPCAKES

Fill a piping bag fitted with an Ateco 826 piping tip with the chocolate fudge frosting. Pipe a "rose swirl" (see page 13 for more instructions) of the frosting onto the brownie cupcakes and sprinkle with the rainbow chips.

TAKE ON THESE CARAMEL CORN CUPCAKES

SONG: a-ha—Take On Me (1985)

YIELD: 12 cupcakes

Take on these cupcakes and you won't be disappointed. As they're made with a brown butter cake, salted caramel buttercream and homemade salted caramel sauce, you'll be coming for them, okay? In fact, make two batches because it's better to be safe than sorry, as these cupcakes will be gone in a day or twooooooooo. I wouldn't sell them for all the money in the world. Not for a hundred billion, million, trillion dollars!

BROWN BUTTER CUPCAKES

6 tbsp (85 g/¾ stick) unsalted butter

1¼ cups (156 g) all-purpose flour

1½ tsp (7 g) baking powder

½ tsp salt

¾ cup (150 g) granulated sugar

¼ cup (60 ml) vegetable oil

1 large egg, at room temperature

2 tbsp (30 ml) sour cream, at room temperature

2 tsp (10 ml) vanilla extract

½ cup (120 ml) milk, at room temperature

SALTED CARAMEL BUTTERCREAM FROSTING

1 cup (227 g/2 sticks) unsalted butter, at room temperature

2½ cups (300 g) powdered sugar

1 tsp (5 ml) vanilla extract

¼ tsp salt

¼ cup (60 ml) Sticky Sweet Salted Caramel Sauce (page 144)

1 tbsp (15 ml) heavy cream

ADDITIONAL INGREDIENTS

¼ cup (60 ml) Sticky Sweet Salted Caramel Sauce (page 144)

1 cup (30 g) caramel popcorn

BROWN BUTTER CUPCAKES

In a small saucepan, melt and cook the butter over medium-low heat, stirring occasionally, until it starts to turn light golden-brown. Immediately pour the browned butter into a heatproof bowl, let it cool to room temperature and then chill until firm. Bring the brown butter to room temperature before making the cupcakes.

Preheat the oven to 350°F (177°C). Line a cupcake pan with 12 cupcake liners.

In a medium-sized bowl, whisk together the flour, baking powder and salt. Set aside.

In a large bowl, use an electric mixer to cream together the granulated sugar, brown butter and vegetable oil until creamy. Add the egg, sour cream and vanilla, and mix until smooth. Add half of the flour mixture and mix on low speed until mostly incorporated. Slowly pour in the milk while mixing on low speed and then add the remaining flour mixture and mix until the batter is smooth.

Portion the batter into the cupcake liners about three-quarters full. Bake the cupcakes for 20 minutes, or until their tops bounce back when gently touched. Remove them from the oven and let the cupcakes cool in the pan for 5 minutes, then transfer to a wire rack to cool completely.

SALTED CARAMEL BUTTERCREAM FROSTING

In the bowl of a stand mixer fitted with a paddle attachment, whip the butter on medium-high speed for 5 minutes, or until pale and creamy. Add the powdered sugar and mix on low speed until fully incorporated. Add the vanilla and salt. Drizzle in the salted caramel sauce and heavy cream. Turn the mixer to medium speed and whip the buttercream for 2 to 3 minutes, or until smooth and creamy.

ASSEMBLING THE CUPCAKES

Fill a piping bag fitted with an Ateco 869 piping tip with the salted caramel buttercream. Pipe a "rose swirl" (see page 13 for more instructions) of frosting onto the brown butter cupcakes. Add a drizzle of salted caramel sauce and pile on the caramel popcorn.

SONG: Real Life—Send Me an Angel (1983)

YIELD: 12 cupcakes

IT'S PEANUT BUTTER JELLY TIME CUPCAKES

Do you believe in heaven above? If not, these cupcakes are proof of heaven. Back in the day, PB & J's were made with Wonder® bread, so a white cupcake is totes the way to go. Let's turn up the juice and see what comes loose and fill the cupcakes with homemade raspberry filling. Then, top them with peanut butter buttercream, an extra swirl of raspberry and chopped salted peanuts. All I can say is, send me these cupcakes, right now.

WHITE CUPCAKES

1¼ cups (156 g) all-purpose flour

1½ tsp (7 g) baking powder

½ tsp salt

¾ cup (150 g) granulated sugar

¼ cup (57 g/½ stick) unsalted butter, at room temperature

¼ cup (60 ml) vegetable oil

2 large egg whites, at room temperature

2 tbsp (30 ml) sour cream, at room temperature

2 tsp (10 ml) vanilla extract

½ cup (120 ml) milk, at room temperature

PEANUT BUTTER BUTTERCREAM FROSTING

1 cup (227 g/2 sticks) unsalted butter, at room temperature

¾ cup (194 g) creamy peanut butter

2 cups (240 g) powdered sugar

1 tsp vanilla extract

¼ tsp salt

1 tbsp (15 ml) heavy cream

ADDITIONAL INGREDIENTS

1 batch raspberry Funky Fresh Fruit Filling (page 148)

2 tbsp (16 g) chopped salted peanuts

WHITE CUPCAKES

Preheat the oven to 350°F (177°C). Line a cupcake pan with 12 cupcake liners.

In a medium-sized bowl, whisk together the flour, baking powder and salt. Set aside.

In a large bowl, use an electric mixer to cream together the granulated sugar, butter and vegetable oil until pale and creamy. Add the egg whites, sour cream and vanilla, and mix until smooth. Add half of the flour mixture and mix on low speed until mostly combined. Slowly pour in the milk, continuing to mix on low speed, then add the remaining flour mixture and mix until the batter is smooth.

Portion the cupcake batter into the cupcake liners about three-quarters full. Bake the cupcakes for 20 minutes, or until their tops spring back when gently touched. Remove them from the oven and let the cupcakes cool in the pan for 5 minutes, then transfer to a wire rack to cool completely.

PEANUT BUTTER BUTTERCREAM FROSTING

In the bowl of a stand mixer fitted with a paddle attachment, whip the butter on medium-high speed for 5 minutes, or until pale and creamy. Add the peanut butter and mix to combine. Add the powdered sugar, vanilla and salt, and mix on low speed until well combined. Drizzle in the heavy cream. Scrape the sides and bottom of the bowl as needed. Turn the mixer to medium speed and whip the buttercream for 2 to 3 minutes, or until smooth and creamy.

ASSEMBLING THE CUPCAKES

Core the cupcakes to remove the center. Use a piping bag with the tip cut off to pipe the raspberry filling into the cupcakes. Fill a piping bag fitted with an Ateco 826 piping tip with the peanut butter frosting. Pipe an "ice cream swirl" (see page 15 for more instructions) of buttercream onto the cupcakes. Use a piping bag with the tip cut off to drizzle the remaining raspberry filling onto the cupcakes. Sprinkle with the chopped salted peanuts.

HOSTESS WITH THE MOSTEST CUPCAKES

SONG: The Cars—You Might Think (1984)

YIELD: 14 cupcakes

You might think I'm foolish to create a copycat version of a Hostess cupcake without the classic white swirl. You might think I'm crazy, but all you'll be wanting are these delectable lunchbox favorites. My cupcakes are made with moist chocolate cake and creamy marshmallow cream filling and iced with a rich chocolate fudge frosting. To shake it up and make these treats uniquely styled, a sprinkling of white nonpareil sprinkles replaces the white swirl. Don't let nothing get in the way of you sinking your teeth into this little gem of nostalgia.

CHOCOLATE CUPCAKES

1 cup (125 g) all-purpose flour

1 cup (200 g) granulated sugar

⅓ cup (33 g) dark cocoa powder

1 tsp baking soda

½ tsp baking powder

½ tsp salt

½ cup (120 ml) milk, at room temperature

¼ cup (60 ml) vegetable oil

1 large egg, at room temperature

1 tsp vanilla extract

½ cup (120 ml) boiling water

CHOCOLATE FUDGE FROSTING

1½ cups (250 g) semisweet chocolate chips

1 cup (120 g) powdered sugar

¾ cup (180 ml) heavy cream

½ cup (114 g/1 stick) unsalted butter

1 tsp vanilla extract

¼ tsp salt

MARSHMALLOW CREAM FILLING

¼ cup (57 g/½ stick) unsalted butter, at room temperature

1 cup (100 g) marshmallow fluff

½ cup (60 g) powdered sugar

ADDITIONAL INGREDIENTS

1 tbsp (15 g) white nonpareil sprinkles

CHOCOLATE CUPCAKES

Preheat the oven to 350°F (177°C). Prepare a cupcake pan with 12 cupcake liners, and an additional pan with 2 cupcake liners.

In a large bowl, whisk together the flour, granulated sugar, dark cocoa powder, baking soda, baking powder and salt. Add the milk, vegetable oil, egg and vanilla, and whisk until well combined. Pour in the boiling water and whisk until the batter is smooth.

Pour the cupcake batter into the cupcake liners about two-thirds full. Bake the cupcakes for 20 to 22 minutes, or until their tops spring back when gently touched. Remove them from the oven and let the cupcakes cool in the pans for 5 minutes, then transfer to a wire rack to cool completely.

CHOCOLATE FUDGE FROSTING

In a medium-sized saucepan over medium-low heat, combine the chocolate chips, powdered sugar, heavy cream, butter, vanilla and salt. Stir the mixture occasionally until melted and smooth. Transfer the frosting to a bowl and let it cool to room temperature. Cover and chill in the refrigerator for 2 hours, or until thickened, stirring the chocolate occasionally while chilling to prevent lumps from forming. The frosting is ready when it has the consistency of peanut butter.

MARSHMALLOW CREAM FILLING

In the bowl of a stand mixer fitted with a whisk attachment, whip the butter until creamy. Add the marshmallow fluff and powdered sugar. Mix on low speed until combined and then whip on medium speed for 2 minutes.

ASSEMBLING THE CUPCAKES

Core the center of the cupcakes. Fill the cupcakes with the marshmallow cream filling. Fill a piping bag fitted with a Wilton 1A piping tip with the chocolate fudge frosting. Pipe a "rose swirl" (see page 13 for more instructions) of the frosting onto the cupcakes. Use an offset spatula to create a swirl in the frosting, starting on the edge of the cupcake and swirling into the center. Decorate with the white nonpareil sprinkles.

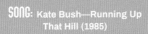

L'EGGO MY CUPCAKES

You'll be running up that road, running up that hill and running up that building to get your hands on these breakfast-inspired cupcakes. Made with maple cinnamon cake, maple cream cheese whipped cream frosting, Stroopwafels, fresh blueberries and a drizzle of maple syrup, these cupcakes will have you levitating, in a good way. Breakfast is the most important meal of the day, so power up like Eleven with these cupcakes so you can fight off the Demogorgon, Mind Flayer and Vecna.

MAPLE CINNAMON CUPCAKES

1¼ cups (156 g) all-purpose flour

1½ tsp (7 g) baking powder

1 tsp ground cinnamon

½ tsp salt

¾ cup (150 g) granulated sugar

¼ cup (57 g/½ stick) unsalted butter, at room temperature

¼ cup (60 ml) vegetable oil

1 large egg, at room temperature

2 tbsp (30 ml) sour cream, at room temperature

2 tbsp (30 ml) pure maple syrup

1 tsp vanilla extract

1 tsp maple extract

⅓ cup (80 ml) milk, at room temperature

MAPLE CREAM CHEESE WHIPPED CREAM FROSTING

8 oz (227 g) cream cheese, cold, cubed

¼ cup (30 g) powdered sugar

¼ cup (60 ml) pure maple syrup

1 tsp vanilla extract

1¼ cups (300 ml) heavy cream

ADDITIONAL INGREDIENTS

3 Stroopwafels, cut into quarters

36 fresh blueberries

2 tbsp (30 ml) pure maple syrup

MAPLE CINNAMON CUPCAKES

Preheat the oven to 350°F (177°C). Line a cupcake pan with 12 cupcake liners.

In a medium-sized bowl, whisk together the flour, baking powder, cinnamon and salt. Set aside.

In a large bowl, cream together the granulated sugar, butter and vegetable oil with an electric mixer until pale and creamy. Add the egg, sour cream, maple syrup, vanilla and maple extract, and mix until smooth. Add half of the flour mixture and mix on low speed until mostly combined. Slowly pour in the milk and then add the remaining flour mixture and mix until the batter is smooth.

Portion the cupcake batter into the cupcake liners about three-quarters full. Bake the cupcakes for 20 minutes, or until their tops bounce back when gently touched. Remove them from the oven and let the cupcakes cool in the pan for 5 minutes, then transfer to a wire rack to cool completely.

MAPLE CREAM CHEESE WHIPPED CREAM FROSTING

In the bowl of a stand mixer fitted with the whisk attachment, whip the cream cheese until smooth. Add the powdered sugar, maple syrup and vanilla, and mix until well combined. Increase the speed to medium and drizzle in the heavy cream. Scrape the sides and bottom of the bowl. Increase the speed to medium-high and whip the frosting until it becomes light and fluffy.

ASSEMBLING THE CUPCAKES

Fill a piping bag fitted with an Ateco 826 piping tip with the whipped cream frosting. Pipe an "ice cream swirl" (see page 15 for more instructions) of the whipped cream onto the cupcakes. Decorate the cupcakes with Stroopwafels and fresh blueberries. Drizzle the maple syrup over the cupcakes immediately before serving.

DREAMY DREAMSICLE CUPCAKES

SONG: Orchestral Manoeuvres in the Dark—If You Leave (1986)

YIELD: 12 cupcakes

If you leave, please don't take my cupcakes away. Promise me just one more cupcake, and make it a dreamsicle cupcake. Modeled after a favorite ice cream novelty, these cupcakes are fluffy and frosted with a swirled orange and vanilla Swiss meringue buttercream frosting. Every second, every moment, we've got to, we've got to make these last—but they won't!

ORANGE CUPCAKES

1¼ cups (156 g) all-purpose flour

1½ tsp (7 g) baking powder

½ tsp salt

¾ cup (150 g) granulated sugar

¼ cup (57 g/½ stick) unsalted butter, at room temperature

¼ cup (60 ml) vegetable oil

1 large egg, at room temperature

2 tbsp (30 ml) sour cream, at room temperature

2 tsp (10 ml) orange extract

1 tsp vanilla extract

½ cup (120 ml) milk, at room temperature

Drop of orange gel food coloring

DREAMSICLE SWISS MERINGUE BUTTERCREAM FROSTING

3 large egg whites, at room temperature

½ cup (100 g) granulated sugar

¼ tsp salt

1¼ cups (284 g/2½ sticks) unsalted butter, at room temperature

2 tsp (10 ml) vanilla extract

1 tsp orange extract

1 to 2 drops orange gel food coloring

ADDITIONAL INGREDIENTS

1 tbsp (15 g) white nonpareil sprinkles

12 orange slices

ORANGE CUPCAKES

Preheat the oven to 350°F (177°C). Line a cupcake pan with 12 cupcake liners.

In a medium-sized bowl, whisk together the flour, baking powder and salt. Set aside.

In a large bowl, cream together the granulated sugar, butter and vegetable oil with an electric mixer until light and creamy. Add the egg, sour cream, orange extract and vanilla, and mix on medium speed until smooth. Add half of the flour mixture and mix on low speed until incorporated. Slowly pour in the milk while mixing on low speed. Add the remaining flour mixture and one drop of orange gel food coloring, and mix until the batter is smooth.

Portion the cupcake batter into the cupcake liners about three-quarters full. Bake the cupcakes for 20 minutes, or until their tops bounce back when gently touched. Remove them from the oven and let the cupcakes cool in the pan for 5 minutes, then transfer to a wire rack to cool completely.

DREAMSICLE SWISS MERINGUE BUTTERCREAM FROSTING

In a heatproof bowl over a pot of simmering water on the stovetop, whisk together the egg whites, granulated sugar and salt. The water should not touch the bowl. Gently heat the mixture, whisking constantly, until the sugar granules are dissolved. Transfer the egg white mixture to the bowl of a stand mixer fitted with a whisk attachment. Whip the egg whites on medium-high speed until they reach glossy, stiff peaks. Turn the mixer to low speed and add the room temperature butter, 1 tablespoon (14 g) at a time. Add the vanilla. Turn the mixer to medium-high speed and whip the buttercream for 5 to 10 minutes, or until smooth and creamy.

Divide the buttercream in half. To one portion, add the orange extract and one to two drops of orange gel food coloring. Mix until well combined and smooth. Leave the remaining vanilla buttercream as it is.

ASSEMBLING THE CUPCAKES

Fill a piping bag fitted with an Ateco 826 piping tip with the Swiss meringue buttercream. Add the orange buttercream to one side of the piping bag and the vanilla buttercream on the other side to create a swirl pattern. Pipe an "ice cream swirl" (see page 15 for more instructions) of frosting onto the cupcakes and decorate with white nonpareil sprinkles and orange slices.

BREAKFAST CLUB CUPCAKES

As you walk on by, will you snatch one of these cupcakes, or will you walk away? Their vibe is Saturday morning ThunderCats and a big bowl of cereal brought to you by Toucan Sam. The cake is made with cereal milk and studded with fruity cereal. Adding a generous swirl of fruity cereal buttercream will have you following your nose and throwing your fist to the sky. Whatever you do, don't you forget about these cupcakes, because you'll need a snack if you ever get Saturday detention.

FRUITY CEREAL CUPCAKES

⅔ cup (160 ml) milk, at room temperature

½ cup (14 g) whole fruity cereal (I prefer Froot Loops®), plus ¼ cup (12 g) roughly chopped fruity cereal

1¼ cups (156 g) all-purpose flour

1½ tsp (7 g) baking powder

½ tsp salt

¾ cup (150 g) granulated sugar

¼ cup (57 g/½ stick) unsalted butter, at room temperature

¼ cup (60 ml) vegetable oil

1 large egg, at room temperature

2 tbsp (30 ml) sour cream, at room temperature

2 tsp (10 ml) vanilla extract

FRUITY CEREAL BUTTERCREAM FROSTING

1 cup (227 g/2 sticks) unsalted butter, at room temperature

2½ cups (300 g) powdered sugar

1 tsp vanilla extract

¼ tsp salt

2 tbsp (30 ml) heavy cream

½ cup (40 g) finely crushed fruity cereal

ADDITIONAL INGREDIENTS

½ cup (25 g) fruity cereal

FRUITY CEREAL CUPCAKES

Preheat the oven to 350°F (177°C). Line two cupcake pans with 12 or 13 cupcake liners.

To make the cereal milk, combine the milk and whole fruity cereal. Let the mixture stand for 20 minutes. Strain the milk from the cereal and save ½ cup of the milk. Discard the cereal and any extra milk.

In a medium-sized bowl, whisk together the flour, baking powder and salt. Set aside.

In a large bowl, use an electric hand mixer to cream together the granulated sugar, butter and vegetable oil until smooth. Add the egg, sour cream and vanilla. Mix on medium speed until well combined. Add half of the flour mixture and mix on low speed. Slowly pour in the cereal milk and then the remaining flour mixture, then mix until the batter is smooth. Fold in the chopped fruity cereal.

Portion the cupcake batter into the cupcake liners about three-quarters full. Bake the cupcakes for 20 minutes, or until their tops bounce back when gently touched. Remove them from the oven and let the cupcakes cool in the pans for 5 minutes, then transfer to a wire rack to cool completely.

FRUITY CEREAL BUTTERCREAM FROSTING

In the bowl of a stand mixer fitted with a paddle attachment, whip the butter on medium-high speed for 5 minutes, or until pale and creamy. Add the powdered sugar and mix on low speed until incorporated. Add the vanilla and salt, and drizzle in the heavy cream. Scrape the sides and bottom of the bowl as needed. Add the finely crushed fruity cereal. Turn the mixer to medium speed and whip the buttercream for 2 to 3 minutes, or until light and creamy.

ASSEMBLING THE CUPCAKES

Fill a piping bag fitted with an Ateco 826 piping tip with the fruity cereal buttercream. Pipe an "ice cream swirl" (see page 15 for more instructions) of the frosting onto the cupcakes and decorate with fruity cereal.

FANTABULOUS FLUFFERNUTTER CUPCAKES

SONG: Ray Parker Jr.—
Ghostbusters (1984)

YIELD: 12 cupcakes

Who you gonna call? Me, to thank me for sharing this delicious recipe that is ooey and gooey. These cupcakes are made with white cake, marshmallow cream, peanut butter buttercream frosting and, of course, more marshmallows. I suggest staying true to the movie and using Stay Puft marshmallows, but you can use whatever brand your ghostly heart desires. Slimer himself would be gobbling these up. These cupcakes will take you from saying "I am the Gatekeeper" to "I am the baker!"

WHITE CUPCAKES

1¼ cups (156 g) all-purpose flour

1½ tsp (7 g) baking powder

½ tsp salt

¾ cup (150 g) granulated sugar

¼ cup (57 g/½ stick) unsalted butter, at room temperature

¼ cup (60 ml) vegetable oil

2 large egg whites, at room temperature

2 tbsp (30 ml) sour cream, at room temperature

2 tsp (10 ml) vanilla extract

½ cup (120 ml) milk, at room temperature

PEANUT BUTTER BUTTERCREAM FROSTING

1 cup (227 g/2 sticks) unsalted butter, at room temperature

¾ cup (194 g) creamy peanut butter

2 cups (240 g) powdered sugar

1 tsp vanilla extract

¼ tsp salt

1 tbsp (15 ml) heavy cream

MARSHMALLOW CREAM FILLING

¼ cup (57 g/½ stick) unsalted butter, at room temperature

1 cup (100 g) marshmallow fluff

½ cup (60 g) powdered sugar

½ tsp vanilla extract

ADDITIONAL INGREDIENTS

2 tbsp (32 g) peanut butter, melted

2 tbsp (16 g) salted peanuts, chopped

36 mini marshmallows, toasted with a kitchen torch

WHITE CUPCAKES

Preheat the oven to 350°F (177°C). Line a cupcake pan with 12 cupcake liners.

In a medium-sized bowl, whisk together the flour, baking powder and salt. Set aside.

In a large bowl, use an electric hand mixer to cream together the granulated sugar, butter and vegetable oil until pale and creamy. Add the egg whites, sour cream and vanilla, and mix until smooth. Add half of the flour mixture to the batter and mix on low speed until mostly combined. Slowly pour in the milk, continuing to mix on low speed. Add the remaining flour mixture and mix until the batter is smooth.

Portion the cupcake batter into the cupcake liners about three-quarters full. Bake the cupcakes for 20 minutes, or until their tops bounce back when gently touched. Remove them from the oven and let the cupcakes cool in the pan for 5 minutes, then transfer to a wire rack to cool completely.

PEANUT BUTTER BUTTERCREAM FROSTING

In the bowl of a stand mixer fitted with a paddle attachment, whip the butter on medium-high speed for 5 minutes, or until pale and creamy. Add the peanut butter and mix to combine. Add the powdered sugar, vanilla and salt. Mix on low speed until well combined. Slowly drizzle in the heavy cream. Scrape the sides and bottom of the bowl as needed. Turn the mixer to medium speed and whip the buttercream for 2 to 3 minutes, or until smooth and creamy.

MARSHMALLOW CREAM FILLING

In the bowl of a stand mixer fitted with a whisk attachment, whip the butter until smooth and creamy. Add the marshmallow fluff, powdered sugar and vanilla. Mix on low speed until combined and then turn the mixer to medium speed and whip for 2 minutes.

ASSEMBLING THE CUPCAKES

Core the cupcakes to remove the center. Use a piping bag with the tip cut off to fill the cupcakes with the marshmallow cream filling. Fill a piping bag fitted with an Ateco 826 piping tip with the peanut butter frosting. Pipe an "ice cream swirl" (see page 15 for more instructions) of buttercream onto the cupcakes. Drizzle the cupcakes with melted peanut butter, then add the chopped salted peanuts and toasted mini marshmallows.

WHERE CAN I FIND A COOKIE
Like That?

If you're a real tough cookie, you will love this chapter. I mean, who doesn't love cookies? No trip to the mall was complete without a stop at Suncoast Motion Picture Company for the latest movie release and Mrs. Fields® for a soft and chewy chocolate chip cookie. Perhaps you were a Girl Scout trying to earn badges by selling Thin Mints® and Do-si-dos®? Or better yet, your zany inventor father created a shrink ray that miniaturized you and the neighbors' kids and you had to venture your way through a treacherous backyard and battle an ant for the rights over an oatmeal creme pie. No matter what your adventure looked like back then, it's safe to say that we all loved cookies.

In this chapter, I will share with you cookielicious cupcakes inspired by classic cookie favorites. Chocolate lovers will be stoked with the ubiquitous chocolate chip cookie (page 63) and chocolate sandwich cookie cupcakes (page 64). If cinnamon and spice make you feel nice, give the caramelized cookie and snickerdoodle cupcakes (pages 67 and 71) a whirl. And if your love language is rainbow sprinkles, bake up some circus animal cookie or sprinkle cookie cupcakes (pages 72 and 68) with cake batter buttercream frosting. With these recipes, we don't need to decide whether cupcakes or cookies are the better treat. Why not have it all?

SONG: Eddie Money—Take Me
Home Tonight (1986)

YIELD: 12 to 14 cupcakes

CENTERFOLD CHOCOLATE CHIP COOKIE CUPCAKES

I feel a hunger; it's a hunger for chocolate chip cookies. So let's cake me home tonight and turn them into cupcakes. These cupcakes are made with brown sugar chocolate chip cake, cookie dough buttercream frosting and mini chocolate chips, and topped with a chocolate chip cookie. Anticipation is running through me and I can feel your heart beat faster thinking about taking one home tonight. So, be my little baker and make these delicious cupcakes.

CHOCOLATE CHIP CUPCAKES

1¼ cups (156 g) all-purpose flour

1½ tsp (7 g) baking powder

½ tsp salt

½ cup (110 g) packed light brown sugar

¼ cup (50 g) granulated sugar

¼ cup (57 g/½ stick) unsalted butter, at room temperature

¼ cup (60 ml) vegetable oil

1 large egg, at room temperature

2 tbsp (30 ml) sour cream, at room temperature

2 tsp (10 ml) vanilla extract

½ cup (120 ml) milk, at room temperature

¼ cup (48 g) mini chocolate chips

COOKIE DOUGH BUTTERCREAM FROSTING

½ cup (63 g) all-purpose flour

1 cup (227 g/2 sticks) unsalted butter, at room temperature

½ cup (110 g) packed light brown sugar

1½ cups (180 g) powdered sugar

2 tsp (10 ml) vanilla extract

½ tsp salt

3 tbsp (45 ml) heavy cream

ADDITIONAL INGREDIENTS

2 tbsp (24 g) mini chocolate chips

12 to 14 mini chocolate chip cookies

CHOCOLATE CHIP CUPCAKES

Preheat the oven to 350°F (177°C). Line two cupcake pans with 12 to 14 cupcake liners.

In a medium-sized bowl, whisk together the flour, baking powder and salt. Set aside.

In a large bowl, cream together the brown sugar, granulated sugar, butter and vegetable oil with an electric mixer until smooth. Add the egg, sour cream and vanilla, and mix well. Add half of the flour mixture to the batter and mix on low speed until incorporated. Slowly pour in the milk, then add the remaining flour mixture and mix until the batter is smooth. Fold in the mini chocolate chips.

Portion the cupcake batter into the cupcake liners about three-quarters full. Bake the cupcakes for 20 minutes, or until their tops bounce back when gently touched. Remove them from the oven and let the cupcakes cool in the pans for 5 minutes, then transfer to a wire rack to cool completely.

COOKIE DOUGH BUTTERCREAM FROSTING

In a microwave-safe bowl, heat the flour in the microwave for 1 minute, stirring every 15 seconds. Set aside to cool.

In the bowl of a stand mixer fitted with a paddle attachment, cream the butter for 5 minutes, or until pale and creamy. Add the brown sugar and whip for an additional 5 minutes. Add the heat-treated flour, powdered sugar, vanilla and salt, and mix on low speed until combined. Drizzle in the heavy cream. Turn the mixer to medium speed and whip for an additional 3 minutes, or until the frosting is light and creamy.

ASSEMBLING THE CUPCAKES

Fill a piping bag fitted with an Ateco 826 piping tip with the cookie dough buttercream. Pipe an "ice cream swirl" (see page 15 for more instructions) of the frosting onto the cupcakes. Sprinkle mini chocolate chips onto the frosting and top each cupcake with a mini chocolate chip cookie.

MILK'S FAVORITE COOKIE CUPCAKES

SONG: Jackson Browne—
Somebody's Baby (1982)

YIELD: 12 cupcakes

I try to shut my eyes, but I can't get these cupcakes out of my sight. Is there a more nostalgic cookie than an O-R-E-O? Whether you dunk your cookie into a glass of milk or twist it open and lick the cream filling, these cookies are always a winner. To replicate that classic Oreo taste, we will be making the cupcakes with black cocoa powder for an intense chocolate flavor. A generous swirl of cookies and cream buttercream frosting, a drizzle of chocolate ganache and chocolate sandwich cookies amp up the goodness. These cupcakes will fill the void in our hearts for the Oreo Big Stuf and are gonna shine tonight.

BLACK COCOA CUPCAKES
¾ cup (180 ml) boiling water

¼ cup (42 g) dark chocolate chips

¼ cup (25 g) black cocoa powder

¾ cup (94 g) all-purpose flour

¾ cup (150 g) granulated sugar

½ tsp baking soda

½ tsp salt

⅓ cup (80 ml) vegetable oil

2 large eggs, at room temperature

1 tsp vanilla extract

4 chocolate sandwich cookies (I prefer Oreo brand), chopped

COOKIES AND CREAM BUTTERCREAM FROSTING
1 cup (227 g/2 sticks) unsalted butter, at room temperature

2½ cups (300 g) powdered sugar

2 tsp (10 ml) vanilla extract

¼ tsp salt

2 tbsp (30 ml) heavy cream

½ cup (60 g) chocolate sandwich cookie crumbs

ADDITIONAL INGREDIENTS
1 batch Most Excellent Chocolate Ganache Drizzle (page 143)

6 chocolate sandwich cookies, halved

BLACK COCOA CUPCAKES
Preheat the oven to 350°F (177°C). Prepare a cupcake pan with 12 cupcake liners.

In a medium-sized bowl, stir together the boiling water, chocolate chips and black cocoa powder until the chocolate chips melt and the cocoa dissolves. Set aside to cool for 5 minutes.

In a large bowl, whisk together the flour, granulated sugar, baking soda and salt. Pour in the cooled chocolate mixture and whisk until well combined. Add the vegetable oil, eggs and vanilla. Whisk until the batter is combined and smooth. Fold in the chopped chocolate sandwich cookies.

Pour the cupcake batter into the cupcake liners about two-thirds full. Bake the cupcakes for 20 minutes, or until their tops spring back when gently touched. Remove them from the oven and let the cupcakes cool in the pan for 5 minutes, then transfer to a wire rack to cool completely.

COOKIES AND CREAM BUTTERCREAM FROSTING
In the bowl of a stand mixer fitted with a paddle attachment, whip the butter on medium-high speed for 5 minutes, or until pale and creamy. Add the powdered sugar and mix on low speed until fully incorporated with the butter. Add the vanilla and salt. Slowly drizzle in the heavy cream until fully incorporated and then add the chocolate sandwich cookie crumbs. Scrape the sides and bottom of the bowl as needed. Turn the mixer to medium speed and whip the buttercream for 2 to 3 minutes, or until smooth and creamy.

ASSEMBLING THE CUPCAKES
Fill a piping bag fitted with an Ateco 826 piping tip with the cookies and cream buttercream. Pipe an "ice cream swirl" (see page 15 for more instructions) of frosting onto the cupcakes. Drizzle the chocolate ganache over the cupcakes and add one-half chocolate sandwich cookie to each cupcake.

SONG: Robert Palmer—Simply Irresistible (1988)

YIELD: 12 cupcakes

SUGAR AND SPICE COOKIE CUPCAKES

How can these cupcakes be permissible with so much cookie butter packed in? These cupcakes are made with caramel cookie crumbs, swirled with caramel cookie butter buttercream frosting, drizzled with cookie butter and topped with a caramel cookie. I don't think you could stuff more cookie butter goodness into these cupcakes if you were double dog dared. It's inconceivable! They are a craze I'd endorse and a powerful force, and I find them simply irresistible.

CARAMEL COOKIE CUPCAKES

1¼ cups (156 g) all-purpose flour

¼ cup (25 g) finely crushed caramel cookies (I prefer Biscoff® brand)

1½ tsp (7 g) baking powder

½ tsp salt

¾ cup (150 g) granulated sugar

¼ cup (57 g/½ stick) unsalted butter, at room temperature

¼ cup (60 ml) vegetable oil

1 large egg, at room temperature

2 tbsp (30 ml) sour cream, at room temperature

2 tsp (10 ml) vanilla extract

½ cup (120 ml) milk, at room temperature

COOKIE BUTTER BUTTERCREAM FROSTING

1 cup (227 g/2 sticks) unsalted butter, at room temperature

⅓ cup (80 g) caramel cookie butter (I prefer Biscoff brand)

2½ cups (300 g) powdered sugar

2 tsp (10 ml) vanilla extract

¼ tsp salt

2 tbsp (30 ml) heavy cream

ADDITIONAL INGREDIENTS

¼ cup (60 g) caramel cookie butter

6 caramel cookies, halved

1 tbsp (6 g) caramel cookie crumbs

CARAMEL COOKIE CUPCAKES

Preheat the oven to 350°F (177°C). Line a cupcake pan with 12 cupcake liners.

In a medium-sized bowl, whisk together the flour, caramel cookie crumbs, baking powder and salt. Set aside.

In a large bowl, use an electric hand mixer to cream the granulated sugar, butter, and vegetable oil until pale and creamy. Add the egg, sour cream and vanilla, and mix on medium speed until smooth. Add half of the flour mixture to the batter and mix on low speed until mostly combined. Slowly pour in the milk while continuing to mix on low speed. Add the remaining flour mixture and mix until the batter is smooth.

Portion the cupcake batter into the cupcake liners about three-quarters full. Bake the cupcakes for 20 minutes, or until their tops bounce back when gently touched. Remove them from the oven and let the cupcakes cool in the pan for 5 minutes, then transfer to a wire rack to cool completely.

COOKIE BUTTER BUTTERCREAM FROSTING

In the bowl of a stand mixer fitted with a paddle attachment, whip the butter on medium-high speed for 5 minutes, or until pale and creamy. Add the caramel cookie butter and mix until thoroughly incorporated with the butter. Add the powdered sugar and mix on low speed until fully incorporated. Add the vanilla and salt. Slowly drizzle in the heavy cream. Scrape the sides and bottom of the bowl as needed. Turn the mixer to medium speed and whip the buttercream for 2 to 3 minutes, or until smooth and creamy.

ASSEMBLING THE CUPCAKES

Fill a piping bag fitted with a Wilton 1M piping tip with the buttercream. Pipe an "ice cream swirl" (see page 15 for more instructions) of buttercream onto the cupcakes. In a microwave-safe bowl, melt the cookie butter in a microwave for 15 seconds. Drizzle the cookie butter over the frosted cupcakes and top each cupcake with one-half of a caramel cookie and sprinkle with caramel cookie crumbs.

SIXTEEN CANDLES SPRINKLE COOKIE CUPCAKES

SONG: Spandau Ballet—True (1083)

YIELD: 12 cupcakes

What's happenin', hot stuff? If you made a wish for sprinkle cookie deliciousness, it already came true. You will be head over heels when you are toe to toe with these sprinkle cookie cupcakes. They taste like the best birthday cake you've ever had swirled with birthday cake buttercream frosting. Adding a rainbow sprinkled birthday cake cookie is the perfect crown for this little masterpiece. I know this much is true: By night's end, I predict you and these cupcakes will interface.

BIRTHDAY CAKE CUPCAKES

¾ cup (94 g) all-purpose flour

½ cup (80 g) white cake mix

½ tsp salt

½ cup (100 g) granulated sugar

¼ cup (57 g/½ stick) unsalted butter, at room temperature

¼ cup (60 ml) vegetable oil

1 large egg, at room temperature

2 tbsp (30 ml) sour cream, at room temperature

2 tsp (10 ml) vanilla extract

⅓ cup (80 ml) milk, at room temperature

2 tbsp (30 g) rainbow sprinkles

CAKE BATTER BUTTERCREAM FROSTING

¾ cup (120 g) white cake mix

1 cup (227 g/2 sticks) unsalted butter, at room temperature

2½ cups (300 g) powdered sugar

2 tsp (10 ml) vanilla extract

¼ tsp salt

2 tbsp (30 ml) heavy cream

ADDITIONAL INGREDIENTS

1 tbsp (15 g) rainbow nonpareil sprinkles

12 mini sprinkle cookies

BIRTHDAY CAKE CUPCAKES

Preheat the oven to 350°F (177°C). Line a cupcake pan with 12 cupcake liners.

In a medium-sized bowl, whisk together the flour, white cake mix and salt. Set aside.

In a large bowl, cream the granulated sugar, butter and vegetable oil with an electric mixer until pale and creamy. Add the egg, sour cream and vanilla, and mix until smooth. Add half of the flour mixture to the batter and mix on low speed until mostly combined. Slowly pour in the milk, then add the remaining flour mixture and mix until the batter is smooth. Fold in the rainbow sprinkles.

Portion the cupcake batter into the cupcake liners about two-thirds full. Bake the cupcakes for 20 minutes, or until their tops bounce back when gently touched. Remove them from the oven and let the cupcakes cool in the pan for 5 minutes, then transfer to a wire rack to cool completely.

CAKE BATTER BUTTERCREAM FROSTING

In a microwave-safe bowl, heat the white cake mix in a microwave for 1 minute, stirring every 15 seconds. Set aside to cool.

In the bowl of a stand mixer fitted with a paddle attachment, whip the butter on medium-high speed for 5 minutes, or until pale and creamy. Add the powdered sugar and white cake mix, and mix on low speed until fully incorporated with the butter. Add the vanilla and salt. Slowly drizzle in the heavy cream until fully incorporated. Turn the mixer to medium speed and whip the buttercream for 2 to 3 minutes, or until light and creamy.

ASSEMBLING THE CUPCAKES

Fill a piping bag fitted with a Wilton 1M piping tip with the cake batter buttercream. Pipe an "ice cream swirl" (see page 15 for more instructions) of frosting onto the cupcakes. Decorate the cupcakes with rainbow nonpareil sprinkles and sprinkle cookies.

SMOOTH CRIMINAL SNICKERDOODLE CUPCAKES

I like the feeling these cupcakes are giving me. They are made with a tender cinnamon sugar cupcake, iced with cinnamon cream cheese frosting and dusted with even more cinnamon sugar. Take my strong advice and remove your sequined glove for this recipe. Not only will these sweet treats give you a fever like you've never ever known, they will have you moonwalking like a smooth criminal across your kitchen.

CINNAMON SUGAR CUPCAKES

1¼ cups (156 g) all-purpose flour

¾ tsp cream of tartar

½ tsp salt

1 tsp ground cinnamon, divided

¼ tsp baking soda

¾ cup (150 g) + 2 tbsp (30 g) granulated sugar, divided

¼ cup (57 g/½ stick) unsalted butter, at room temperature

¼ cup (60 ml) vegetable oil

1 large egg, at room temperature

1 large egg white, at room temperature

2 tsp (10 ml) vanilla extract

½ cup (120 ml) buttermilk, at room temperature

CINNAMON CREAM CHEESE FROSTING

¾ cup (170 g/1½ sticks) unsalted butter, at room temperature

4 oz (113 g) cream cheese, at room temperature

2½ cups (300 g) powdered sugar

2 tsp (10 ml) vanilla extract

½ tsp ground cinnamon

¼ tsp salt

ADDITIONAL INGREDIENTS

1 tbsp (15 g) granulated sugar

¼ tsp ground cinnamon

12 cinnamon sticks

CINNAMON SUGAR CUPCAKES

Preheat the oven to 350°F (177°C). Line a cupcake pan with 12 cupcake liners.

In a medium-sized bowl, whisk together the flour, cream of tartar, salt, ½ teaspoon of cinnamon and baking soda. Set aside.

In a large bowl, use an electric hand mixer to cream together the ¾ cup (150 g) of granulated sugar, butter and vegetable oil until pale and creamy. Add the egg, egg white and vanilla, and mix until smooth. Add half of the flour mixture and mix on low speed until mostly combined. Slowly pour in the buttermilk, continuing to mix on low speed. Add the remaining flour mixture and mix until the batter is smooth.

Portion the cupcake batter into the cupcake liners about two-thirds full. Stir together the remaining 2 tablespoons (30 g) of granulated sugar and ½ teaspoon of cinnamon to make cinnamon sugar, and sprinkle over the top of the cupcake batter. Bake the cupcakes for 20 minutes, or until their tops bounce back when gently touched. Remove them from the oven and let the cupcakes cool in the pan for 5 minutes, then transfer to a wire rack to cool completely.

CINNAMON CREAM CHEESE FROSTING

In the bowl of a stand mixer fitted with a whisk attachment, whip the butter and cream cheese on medium-high speed until smooth. Add the powdered sugar, vanilla, cinnamon and salt. Mix on low speed until combined. Turn the mixer to medium-high speed and whip the frosting for an additional 2 to 3 minutes, or until smooth and creamy. Scrape the sides and bottom of the bowl as needed.

ASSEMBLING THE CUPCAKES

Fill a piping bag fitted with a Wilton 2D piping tip with the cinnamon cream cheese frosting. Pipe an "ice cream swirl" (see page 15 for more instructions) of frosting onto the cupcakes. Stir together the granulated sugar and cinnamon to make cinnamon sugar. Sprinkle the cupcakes with the cinnamon sugar and decorate with the cinnamon sticks.

STARDUST CIRCUS ANIMAL COOKIE CUPCAKES

SONG: David Bowie—Let's Dance (1983)

YIELD: 12 cupcakes

Let's bake! Put on your red shoes and bake the blues to the song they're playing on the radio (obviously '80s hits). These cupcakes remind me of the cookie (what cookie?), cookie with the sprinkles (what sprinkles?), sprinkles of voodoo (who do?), you do (do what?), remind me of circus animal cookies. These pink-swirled cupcakes have chunks of circus animal cookies baked in and are iced with circus animal cookie buttercream frosting. You may never fall for modern love, but you will certainly fall for these cupcakes.

CIRCUS ANIMAL CUPCAKES

1¼ cups (156 g) all-purpose flour

1½ tsp (7 g) baking powder

½ tsp salt

¾ cup (150 g) granulated sugar

¼ cup (57 g/½ stick) unsalted butter, at room temperature

¼ cup (60 ml) vegetable oil

2 large egg whites, at room temperature

2 tbsp (30 ml) sour cream, at room temperature

1 tsp vanilla extract

1 tsp almond extract

½ cup (120 ml) milk, at room temperature

1 drop of pink gel food coloring

¼ cup (40 g) finely chopped circus animal cookies

CIRCUS ANIMAL COOKIE BUTTERCREAM FROSTING

1 cup (227 g/2 sticks) unsalted butter, at room temperature

2½ cups (300 g) powdered sugar

2 tsp (10 ml) vanilla extract

¼ tsp salt

2 tbsp (30 ml) heavy cream

½ cup (70 g) finely ground circus animal cookie crumbs

ADDITIONAL INGREDIENTS

1 tbsp (15 g) rainbow nonpareil sprinkles

12 frosted circus animal cookies

CIRCUS ANIMAL CUPCAKES

Preheat the oven to 350°F (177°C). Line a cupcake pan with 12 cupcake liners.

In a medium-sized bowl, whisk together the flour, baking powder and salt. Set aside.

In a large bowl, use an electric hand mixer to cream together the granulated sugar, butter and vegetable oil until creamy. Add the egg whites, sour cream, vanilla and almond extract, and mix until smooth. Add half of the flour mixture to the batter and mix on low speed until incorporated. Slowly pour in the milk and then add the remaining flour mixture, and mix until the batter is smooth. Divide the batter in half. Tint one portion with a drop of pink gel food coloring. To the other half, fold in the finely chopped animal cookies.

Alternate adding small spoonfuls of the pink and circus animal cookie cupcake batter into the cupcake liners until they are about three-quarters full. Bake the cupcakes for 20 minutes, or until their tops bounce back when gently touched. Remove them from the oven and let the cupcakes cool in the pan for 5 minutes, then transfer to a wire rack to cool completely.

CIRCUS ANIMAL COOKIE BUTTERCREAM FROSTING

In the bowl of a stand mixer fitted with a paddle attachment, whip the butter on medium-high speed for 5 minutes, or until pale and creamy. Add the powdered sugar and mix on low speed until fully incorporated. Add the vanilla and salt, and then slowly drizzle in the heavy cream. Add the circus animal cookie crumbs. Turn the mixer to medium speed and whip the buttercream for 2 to 3 minutes, or until smooth and creamy.

ASSEMBLING THE CUPCAKES

Fill a piping bag fitted with an Ateco 826 piping tip with the circus animal cookie buttercream. Pipe an "ice cream swirl" (see page 15 for more instructions) of the frosting onto the cupcakes. Sprinkle the cupcakes with rainbow nonpareil sprinkles and top each cupcake with a circus animal cookie.

SONG: The Romantics—Talking in Your Sleep (1983)

YIELD: 12 cupcakes

MAD ABOUT MINT CHOCOLATE COOKIE CUPCAKES

When you close your eyes and go to sleep, you will be dreaming of these mint chocolate cookie cupcakes. Hopefully, no one wakes you up by holding a boom box over their head outside your window. There is no better way to earn your cookie business patch than with these cupcakes made with mint chocolate cake and bits of mint chocolate cookies baked right in. A swirl of mint buttercream frosting, cookie crumbs and a mint chocolate cookie will have you go up, down and jump around. You tell me that you want them, you tell me that you need them, you tell me that you love them, so let's get baking.

MINT CHOCOLATE COOKIE CUPCAKES

¾ cup (180 ml) boiling water

¼ cup (42 g) semisweet or dark chocolate chips

¼ cup (25 g) dark cocoa powder

¾ cup (94 g) all-purpose flour

¾ cup (150 g) granulated sugar

½ tsp baking soda

½ tsp salt

⅓ cup (80 ml) vegetable oil

2 large eggs, at room temperature

1 tsp vanilla extract

½ tsp spearmint extract

4 mint chocolate cookies (I prefer Thin Mints brand), chopped finely

MINT BUTTERCREAM FROSTING

1 cup (227 g/2 sticks) unsalted butter, at room temperature

2½ cups (300 g) powdered sugar

1½ tsp (8 ml) spearmint extract

1 tsp vanilla extract

¼ tsp salt

1 to 2 drops green gel food coloring

2 tbsp (30 ml) heavy cream

ADDITIONAL INGREDIENTS

1 tbsp (8 g) mint chocolate cookie crumbs

6 mint chocolate cookies, halved

Fresh mint leaves

MINT CHOCOLATE COOKIE CUPCAKES

Preheat the oven to 350°F (177°C). Prepare a cupcake pan with 12 cupcake liners.

In a medium-sized bowl, stir together the boiling water, chocolate chips and dark cocoa powder until the chocolate chips are melted. Set aside to cool for 5 minutes.

In a large bowl, whisk together the flour, granulated sugar, baking soda and salt. Pour in the cooled chocolate mixture and whisk until well combined. Add the vegetable oil, eggs, vanilla and spearmint extract. Whisk until combined and smooth. Fold in the chopped mint chocolate cookies.

Pour the cupcake batter into the cupcake liners about two-thirds full. Bake the cupcakes for 20 minutes, or until their tops spring back when touched. Remove them from the oven and let the cupcakes cool in the pan for 5 minutes, then transfer to a wire rack to cool completely.

MINT BUTTERCREAM FROSTING

In the bowl of a stand mixer fitted with a paddle attachment, whip the butter on medium-high speed for 5 minutes, or until pale and creamy. Add the powdered sugar and mix on low speed until fully incorporated. Add the spearmint extract, vanilla, salt and green gel food coloring. Slowly drizzle in the heavy cream. Scrape the sides and bottom of the bowl as needed. Turn the mixer to medium speed and whip the buttercream for 2 to 3 minutes, or until smooth and creamy.

ASSEMBLING THE CUPCAKES

Fill a piping bag fitted with a Wilton 1M piping tip with the mint buttercream. Pipe an "ice cream swirl" (see page 15 for more instructions) of frosting onto the cupcakes. Sprinkle mint chocolate cookie crumbs onto the frosting and garnish each cupcake with one-half mint chocolate cookie and mint leaves.

OATRAGEOUS OATMEAL CREME PIE CUPCAKES

SONG: Rick Astley—Never Gonna Give You Up (1987)

YIELD: 14 cupcakes

We're no strangers to oatmeal creme pies; your heart's been aching for this luscious recipe. You're never gonna give them up, they're never gonna let you down, never gonna run around and DESSERT you. These cupcakes will have you shimmying in a tan trench coat and doing backflips off brick walls. They are made with tender cinnamon molasses cake, iced with marshmallow cream frosting and piled high with oatmeal creme pie pieces. Don't you know, I would move heaven and earth to be together forever with these cupcakes, or at least, journey through a backyard wilderness.

CINNAMON MOLASSES CUPCAKES
1¼ cups (156 g) all-purpose flour

1½ tsp (7 g) baking powder

1 tsp ground cinnamon

½ tsp salt

¾ cup (150 g) granulated sugar

¼ cup (57 g/½ stick) unsalted butter, at room temperature

¼ cup (60 ml) vegetable oil

1 large egg, at room temperature

2 tbsp (30 ml) sour cream, at room temperature

1 tbsp (20 g) molasses

2 tsp (10 ml) vanilla extract

½ cup (120 ml) milk, at room temperature

MARSHMALLOW CREAM FROSTING
1 cup (227 g/2 sticks) unsalted butter, at room temperature

2 cups (200 g) marshmallow fluff

1½ cups (180 g) powdered sugar

2 tsp (10 ml) vanilla extract

¼ tsp salt

2 tbsp (30 ml) heavy cream

ADDITIONAL INGREDIENTS
4 oatmeal creme pies

CINNAMON MOLASSES CUPCAKES
Preheat the oven to 350°F (177°C). Line two cupcake pans with 14 cupcake liners.

In a medium-sized bowl, whisk together the flour, baking powder, cinnamon and salt. Set aside.

In a large bowl, cream together the granulated sugar, butter and vegetable oil with an electric mixer until creamy. Add the egg, sour cream, molasses and vanilla. Mix on medium speed until smooth. Add half of the flour mixture and mix on low speed until mostly combined. Slowly pour in the milk, continuing to mix on low speed. Add the remaining flour mixture and mix until the batter is smooth.

Portion the cupcake batter into the cupcake liners about two-thirds full. Bake the cupcakes for 20 minutes, or until their tops bounce back when gently touched. Remove them from the oven and let the cupcakes cool in the pans for 5 minutes, then transfer to a wire rack to cool completely.

MARSHMALLOW CREAM FROSTING
In the bowl of a stand mixer fitted with a paddle attachment, whip the butter on medium-high speed for 5 minutes, or until pale and creamy. Add the marshmallow fluff and mix on low speed until combined with the butter. Add the powdered sugar, vanilla and salt, and mix on low speed until fully incorporated. Drizzle in the heavy cream. Scrape the sides and bottom of the bowl. Turn the mixer to medium speed and whip the frosting for 2 to 3 minutes, or until smooth and creamy.

ASSEMBLING THE CUPCAKES
Fill a piping bag fitted with an Ateco 826 piping tip with the marshmallow cream frosting. Pipe a "double swirl" (see page 13 for more instructions) of frosting onto the cupcakes. Cut the oatmeal creme pies into triangles and add to the top of the marshmallow cream frosting.

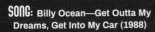

SONG: Billy Ocean—Get Outta My Dreams, Get Into My Car (1988)

YIELD: 12 cupcakes

STRAIGHT UP S'MORES CUPCAKES

Tell these cupcakes to get out of your dreams and into your belly. If you love the taste of s'mores, they will have you dancing on the hood of your grandfather's Cadillac DeVille Sedan. The moist chocolate cakes are topped with graham cracker crunch, iced with toasted marshmallow buttercream and crowned with the classic s'mores trifecta, no campfire required. I feel the need, the need for s'mores.

CHOCOLATE GRAHAM CRACKER CUPCAKES

½ cup (60 g) graham cracker crumbs

2 tbsp (28 g) unsalted butter, melted

1 tbsp (15 g) granulated sugar

¾ cup (180 ml) boiling water

¼ cup (42 g) semisweet or dark chocolate chips

¼ cup (25 g) dark cocoa powder

¾ cup (94 g) all-purpose flour

¾ cup (150 g) granulated sugar

½ tsp baking soda

½ tsp salt

⅓ cup (80 ml) vegetable oil

2 large eggs, at room temperature

1 tsp vanilla extract

TOASTED MARSHMALLOW BUTTERCREAM FROSTING

2 cups (200 g) marshmallow fluff

1 cup (227 g/2 sticks) unsalted butter, at room temperature

1½ cups (180 g) powdered sugar

2 tsp (10 ml) vanilla extract

¼ tsp salt

2 tbsp (30 ml) heavy cream

ADDITIONAL INGREDIENTS

12 graham cracker pieces

12 chocolate bar pieces

36 mini marshmallows, toasted with a kitchen torch

CHOCOLATE GRAHAM CRACKER CUPCAKES

Preheat the oven to 350°F (177°C). Prepare a cupcake pan with 12 cupcake liners.

In a small bowl, stir together the graham cracker crumbs, melted butter and granulated sugar. Set aside.

In a medium-sized bowl, stir together the boiling water, chocolate chips and dark cocoa powder until the chocolate chips are melted. Set aside to cool for 5 minutes.

In a large bowl, whisk together the flour, granulated sugar, baking soda and salt. Pour in the cooled chocolate mixture and whisk until well combined. Add the vegetable oil, eggs and vanilla. Whisk until smooth.

Pour the cupcake batter into the cupcake liners about two-thirds full. Sprinkle the graham cracker crumbs on top of the cupcake batter. Bake the cupcakes for 20 to 22 minutes, or until their tops spring back when gently touched. Remove them from the oven and let the cupcakes cool in the pan for 5 minutes, then transfer to a wire rack to cool completely.

TOASTED MARSHMALLOW BUTTERCREAM FROSTING

Spread the marshmallow fluff in a thin layer onto a plate. Use a kitchen torch to toast the top of the fluff. Stir the fluff and continue to toast a few more times until it is roasty toasty. If you don't have a kitchen torch, you can spread the fluff on a baking pan and broil it in the oven. Set aside to cool.

In the bowl of a stand mixer fitted with a paddle attachment, whip the butter on medium-high speed for 5 minutes, or until pale and creamy. Add the toasted marshmallow fluff and mix on low speed. Add the powdered sugar, vanilla and salt, and mix on low speed until fully incorporated. Drizzle in the heavy cream. Scrape the sides and bottom of the bowl. Turn the mixer to medium speed and whip the buttercream for 2 to 3 minutes, or until smooth and creamy.

ASSEMBLING THE CUPCAKES

Fill a piping bag fitted with a Wilton 1M piping tip with the toasted marshmallow buttercream frosting. Pipe an "ice cream swirl" (see page 15 for more instructions) of frosting onto the cupcakes. Garnish the cupcakes with graham crackers, chocolate bar pieces and toasted mini marshmallows.

I WANT

Candy

Pour some sugar on these cupcakes in the name of love, because
this chapter is dedicated to all things sticky and sweet. If you want to feel like
a kid in a candy store or an extraterrestrial in a creepy backyard following
a trail of Reese's Pieces®, you must read on. If you want to avoid a risky
trip to Orin Scrivello, DDS, be sure to brush and floss, because
this chapter will surely give you cavities.

Sweet dreams are made of these candy-inspired flavors. Chocoholics will flip
their lids for cupcakes packed with caramel, nougat, peanut butter and peanuts (pages 87, 83 and 88). (We will save the Baby Ruths® for the pool.) If
sugary sweet is more your style, cotton candy and popping candy cupcakes
(pages 91 and 84) will tantalize your taste buds and make you sing "Oh,
sweet cupcake o'mine." Watch your favorite '80s flick with a cupcake piled
high with movie theater candies (page 96), and take a trip to Candyland
with Queen Frostine and Princess Lolly. If you want candy,
you've opened up to the sweetest chapter.

SONG: Bon Jovi—Bad Medicine (1988)

YIELD: 12 cupcakes

SO SATISFYING CANDY BAR CUPCAKES

These cupcakes are like bad medicine, and bad medicine is what you need! If you got a dirty down addiction for all things Snickers®, this recipe will have you on your knees. We start off with dark chocolate cupcakes frosted with creamy peanut butter buttercream frosting. Then, they are drizzled with chocolate ganache and salted caramel sauce, sprinkled with salted peanuts and crowned with a peanutty chocolate nougat bar. Although you might rip your tight spandex glam-rock pants, these cupcakes are worth it.

CHOCOLATE CUPCAKES

¾ cup (180 ml) boiling water

¼ cup (42 g) semisweet or dark chocolate chips

¼ cup (25 g) dark cocoa powder

1 tsp instant espresso powder

¾ cup (94 g) all-purpose flour

¾ cup (150 g) granulated sugar

½ tsp baking soda

½ tsp salt

⅓ cup (80 ml) vegetable oil

2 large eggs, at room temperature

1 tsp vanilla extract

PEANUT BUTTER BUTTERCREAM FROSTING

1 cup (227 g/2 sticks) unsalted butter, at room temperature

¾ cup (194 g) creamy peanut butter

2 cups (240 g) powdered sugar

1 tsp vanilla extract

¼ tsp salt

1 tbsp (15 ml) heavy cream

ADDITIONAL INGREDIENTS

¼ cup (60 ml) Sticky Sweet Salted Caramel Sauce (page 144)

1 batch Most Excellent Chocolate Ganache Drizzle (page 143)

2 tbsp (16 g) chopped salted peanuts

6 fun size peanutty chocolate nougat bars (I prefer Snickers brand), halved

CHOCOLATE CUPCAKES

Preheat the oven to 350°F (177°C). Prepare a cupcake pan with 12 cupcake liners.

In a medium-sized bowl, stir together the boiling water, chocolate chips, dark cocoa powder and instant espresso powder until the chocolate chips are melted. Set aside to cool for 5 minutes.

In a large bowl, whisk together the flour, granulated sugar, baking soda and salt. Pour in the cooled chocolate mixture and whisk until well combined. Add the vegetable oil, eggs and vanilla. Whisk until combined and smooth.

Pour the cupcake batter into the cupcake liners about two-thirds full. Bake the cupcakes for 20 minutes, or until their tops bounce back when gently touched. Remove them from the oven and let the cupcakes cool in the pan for 5 minutes, then transfer to a wire rack to cool completely.

PEANUT BUTTER BUTTERCREAM FROSTING

In the bowl of a stand mixer fitted with a paddle attachment, whip the butter on medium-high speed for 5 minutes, or until pale and creamy. Add the peanut butter and mix to combine. Add the powdered sugar, vanilla and salt, and mix on low speed until well combined. Drizzle in the heavy cream and scrape the sides and bottom of the bowl as needed. Turn the mixer to medium speed and whip the buttercream for 2 to 3 minutes, or until pale and creamy.

ASSEMBLING THE CUPCAKES

Fill a piping bag fitted with a Wilton 2D piping tip with the peanut butter buttercream. Pipe a "ruffle swirl" (see page 15 for more instructions) of frosting onto the cupcakes. Drizzle the salted caramel sauce and chocolate ganache over the buttercream swirl. Top the cupcakes with the chopped salted peanuts and one-half of a small peanutty chocolate nougat bar.

POP GOES THE CUPCAKE

SONG: Bow Wow Wow—I Want Candy (1982)

YIELD: 12 cupcakes

You want candy! These cupcakes are just what the doctor ordered. Psych! Although no doctor would prescribe these for your health, they just might for your happiness. They are made with colorful confetti cake, stuffed with raspberry filling, swirled with creamy vanilla buttercream frosting and covered with crackly popping candies. They are everything you desire and so sweet they'll make your mouth water. Whether you are a kid or a kid at heart, these cupcakes are an explosion of deliciousness.

CONFETTI CUPCAKES

1¼ cups (156 g) all-purpose flour

1½ tsp (7 g) baking powder

½ tsp salt

¾ cup (150 g) granulated sugar

¼ cup (57 g/½ stick) unsalted butter, at room temperature

¼ cup (60 ml) vegetable oil

2 large egg whites, at room temperature

2 tbsp (30 ml) sour cream, at room temperature

2 tsp (10 ml) vanilla extract

½ cup (120 ml) milk, at room temperature

¼ cup (45 g) red, white and blue sprinkles

VANILLA BUTTERCREAM FROSTING

1 cup (227 g/2 sticks) unsalted butter, at room temperature

2½ cups (300 g) powdered sugar

2 tsp (10 ml) vanilla extract

¼ tsp salt

2 tbsp (30 ml) heavy cream

ADDITIONAL INGREDIENTS

1 batch raspberry Funky Fresh Fruit Filling (page 148)

12 red, white and blue suckers

2 to 3 packets (20 to 30 g) popping candies (I prefer Pop Rocks® brand)

CONFETTI CUPCAKES

Preheat the oven to 350°F (177°C). Line a cupcake pan with 12 cupcake liners.

In a medium-sized bowl, whisk together the flour, baking powder and salt. Set aside.

In a large bowl, use an electric hand mixer to cream together the granulated sugar, butter and vegetable oil until pale and creamy. Add the egg whites, sour cream and vanilla, and mix until smooth. Add half of the flour mixture to the batter and mix on low speed until mostly combined. Slowly pour in the milk, continuing to mix on low speed. Add the remaining flour mixture and mix until the batter is smooth. Fold in the red, white and blue sprinkles.

Portion the cupcake batter into the cupcake liners about three-quarters full. Bake the cupcakes for 20 minutes, or until their tops bounce back when gently touched. Remove them from the oven and let the cupcakes cool in the pan for 5 minutes, then transfer to a wire rack to cool completely.

VANILLA BUTTERCREAM FROSTING

In the bowl of a stand mixer fitted with a paddle attachment, whip the butter on medium-high speed for 5 minutes, or until pale and creamy. Add the powdered sugar and mix on low speed until fully incorporated. Add the vanilla and salt, and drizzle in the heavy cream. Scrape the sides and bottom of the bowl as needed. Turn the mixer to medium speed and whip the buttercream for 2 to 3 minutes, or until smooth and creamy.

ASSEMBLING THE CUPCAKES

Core the cupcakes to remove the center. Use a piping bag with the tip cut off to fill the cupcakes with the raspberry filling. Fill a piping bag fitted with a Wilton 1M piping tip with the vanilla buttercream. Pipe an "ice cream swirl" (see page 15 for more instructions) of frosting onto the cupcakes. Decorate the cupcakes with a sucker and sprinkle popping candies onto the buttercream immediately before serving.

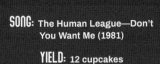

ROLL A CARAMEL CANDY TO YOUR CUPCAKES

Ferris and Sloane, Johnny and Baby, Samantha and Jake. But the best couple award goes to chocolate and caramel! These Rolo®-inspired cupcakes are better than any '80s brat pack movie (or maybe equally as awesome)! Made with moist chocolate cake, salted caramel buttercream frosting, salted caramel sauce, chocolate ganache drizzle, chocolate caramel candy and a sprinkling of flaky sea salt, these cupcakes will give you all the feels as you are watching your favorite John Hughes movie.

CHOCOLATE CUPCAKES

¾ cup (180 ml) boiling water

¼ cup (42 g) semisweet or dark chocolate chips

¼ cup (25 g) dark cocoa powder

1 tsp instant espresso powder

¾ cup (94 g) all-purpose flour

¾ cup (150 g) granulated sugar

½ tsp baking soda

½ tsp salt

⅓ cup (80 ml) vegetable oil

2 large eggs, at room temperature

1 tsp vanilla extract

SALTED CARAMEL BUTTERCREAM FROSTING

1 cup (227 g/2 sticks) unsalted butter, at room temperature

2½ cups (300 g) powdered sugar

1 tsp vanilla extract

¼ tsp salt

¼ cup (60 ml) Sticky Sweet Salted Caramel Sauce (page 144)

1 tbsp (15 ml) heavy cream

ADDITIONAL INGREDIENTS

½ cup (120 ml) Sticky Sweet Salted Caramel Sauce (page 144)

1 batch Most Excellent Chocolate Ganache Drizzle (page 143)

24 chocolate caramel candies (I prefer Rolo brand)

1 tsp flaky sea salt

CHOCOLATE CUPCAKES

Preheat the oven to 350°F (177°C). Line a cupcake pan with 12 cupcake liners.

In a medium-sized bowl, stir together the boiling water, chocolate chips, dark cocoa powder and instant espresso powder until the chocolate chips are melted. Set aside to cool for 5 minutes.

In a large bowl, whisk together the flour, granulated sugar, baking soda and salt. Pour in the cooled chocolate mixture and whisk until well combined. Add the vegetable oil, eggs and vanilla. Whisk until combined and smooth.

Pour the cupcake batter into the cupcake liners about two-thirds full. Bake the cupcakes for 20 minutes, or until their tops spring back when gently touched. Remove them from the oven and let the cupcakes cool in the pan for 5 minutes, then transfer to a wire rack to cool completely.

SALTED CARAMEL BUTTERCREAM FROSTING

In the bowl of a stand mixer fitted with a paddle attachment, whip the butter on medium-high speed for 5 minutes, or until pale and creamy. Add the powdered sugar and mix on low speed until fully incorporated with the butter. Add the vanilla and salt. Drizzle in the salted caramel sauce and heavy cream. Scrape the sides and bottom of the bowl. Turn the mixer to medium speed and whip the buttercream for 2 to 3 minutes, or until smooth and creamy.

ASSEMBLING THE CUPCAKES

Core the cupcakes to remove the center. Use a piping bag with the tip cut off to fill the cupcakes with salted caramel sauce. Fill a piping bag fitted with an Ateco 869 piping tip with the salted caramel buttercream. Pipe an "ice cream swirl" (see page 15 for more instructions) of frosting onto the cupcakes. Add a swirl of chocolate ganache drizzle, chocolate caramel candies and flaky sea salt.

NOBODY BETTER LAY A FINGER ON MY CUPCAKES

SONG: Dead or Alive—You Spin Me Round (Like a Record) (1985)

YIELD: 12 cupcakes

These cupcakes will spin you right round baby right round. They are baked with bits of crispety, crunchety, chocolate peanut buttery candy, iced with peanut butter crunch buttercream frosting and sprinkled with even more Butterfinger® goodness. All I know is that, to me, this recipe is lots of fun, and once you've set your sights on these cupcakes, no other recipe will do.

CHOCOLATE PEANUT BUTTER CRUNCH CUPCAKES

¾ cup (180 ml) boiling water

¼ cup (42 g) semisweet or dark chocolate chips

¼ cup (25 g) dark cocoa powder

¾ cup (94 g) all-purpose flour

¾ cup (150 g) granulated sugar

½ tsp baking soda

½ tsp salt

⅓ cup (80 ml) vegetable oil

2 large eggs, at room temperature

1 tsp vanilla extract

¼ cup (35 g) finely chopped chocolate–peanut butter candy bar (I prefer Butterfinger brand)

PEANUT BUTTER CRUNCH BUTTERCREAM FROSTING

1 cup (227 g/2 sticks) unsalted butter, at room temperature

¾ cup (194 g) creamy peanut butter

2 cups (240 g) powdered sugar

1 tsp vanilla extract

¼ tsp salt

1 tbsp (15 ml) heavy cream

½ cup (65 g) finely crushed chocolate–peanut butter candy bar crumbs

ADDITIONAL INGREDIENTS

¼ cup (35 g) finely crushed chocolate–peanut butter candy bar crumbs

6 fun size chocolate–peanut butter candy bars, halved

CHOCOLATE PEANUT BUTTER CRUNCH CUPCAKES

Preheat the oven to 350°F (177°C). Prepare a cupcake pan with 12 cupcake liners.

In a medium-sized bowl, stir together the boiling water, chocolate chips and dark cocoa powder until the chocolate chips are melted. Set aside to cool for 5 minutes.

In a large bowl, whisk together the flour, granulated sugar, baking soda and salt. Pour in the cooled chocolate mixture and whisk until well combined. Add the vegetable oil, eggs and vanilla, and whisk until the batter is smooth.

Pour the cupcake batter into the cupcake liners about two-thirds full. Sprinkle the finely chopped candy over the cupcake batter. Bake the cupcakes for 20 minutes, or until their tops are set. Remove them from the oven and let the cupcakes cool in the pan for 5 minutes, then transfer to a wire rack to cool completely.

PEANUT BUTTER CRUNCH BUTTERCREAM FROSTING

In the bowl of a stand mixer fitted with a paddle attachment, whip the butter on medium-high speed for 5 minutes, or until pale and creamy. Add the peanut butter and mix to combine. Add the powdered sugar, vanilla and salt, and mix on low speed until combined. Drizzle in the heavy cream. Add the finely crushed candy crumbs. Scrape the sides and bottom of the bowl as needed. Turn the mixer to medium speed and whip the buttercream for 2 to 3 minutes, or until smooth and creamy.

ASSEMBLING THE CUPCAKES

Fill a piping bag fitted with an Ateco 826 piping tip with the peanut butter crunch buttercream. Pipe an "ice cream swirl" (see page 15 for more instructions) of frosting onto the cupcakes. Sprinkle the cupcakes with the finely crushed candy and top each cupcake with one-half of a small chocolate–peanut butter candy bar.

YOU'VE GOT THE FLUFFY STUFF CUPCAKES

First cupcake was a great time, second one was a blast, third one I fell in love and these cupcakes just won't last. They will satisfy your sweet tooth and need for nostalgia. The perfectly pastel pink and blue cotton candy cupcakes are swirled with cotton candy buttercream frosting, and because we don't have enough sugar yet, let's add a puff of cotton candy and cotton candy–flavored Pop Rocks. Step by step, you've gotta get to these cupcakes. You'll really want them in your world.

COTTON CANDY CUPCAKES

1¼ cups (156 g) all-purpose flour

1½ tsp (7 g) baking powder

½ tsp salt

¾ cup (150 g) granulated sugar

¼ cup (57 g/½ stick) unsalted butter, at room temperature

¼ cup (60 ml) vegetable oil

2 large egg whites, at room temperature

2 tbsp (30 ml) sour cream, at room temperature

1½ tsp (8 ml) cotton candy extract

1 tsp vanilla extract

½ cup (120 ml) milk, at room temperature

1 to 2 drops each pink and light blue gel food coloring

COTTON CANDY BUTTERCREAM FROSTING

1 cup (227 g/2 sticks) unsalted butter, at room temperature

2½ cups (300 g) powdered sugar

1 tsp vanilla extract

1 tsp cotton candy extract

¼ tsp salt

2 tbsp (30 ml) heavy cream

1 to 2 drops each pink and light blue gel food coloring

ADDITIONAL INGREDIENTS

2 packets (20 g) cotton candy popping candies (I prefer Pop Rocks brand)

Pink and blue cotton candy

COTTON CANDY CUPCAKES

Preheat the oven to 350°F (177°C). Line a cupcake pan with 12 cupcake liners.

In a medium-sized bowl, whisk together the flour, baking powder and salt. Set aside.

In a large bowl, use an electric hand mixer to cream together the granulated sugar, butter and vegetable oil until pale and creamy. Add the egg whites, sour cream, cotton candy extract and vanilla, and mix on medium speed until smooth. Add half of the flour mixture to the batter and mix on low speed until mostly combined. Slowly pour in the milk, continuing to mix on low speed. Add the remaining flour mixture and mix until smooth.

Divide the cupcake batter in half. Tint one portion of the batter with pink gel food coloring and the other portion with light blue gel food coloring. Add spoonfuls of the pink and blue batter, alternating the colors, into the cupcake liners to about three-quarters full. Bake the cupcakes for 20 minutes, or until their tops bounce back when gently touched. Remove them from the oven and let the cupcakes cool in the pan for 5 minutes, then transfer to a wire rack to cool completely.

COTTON CANDY BUTTERCREAM FROSTING

In the bowl of a stand mixer fitted with a paddle attachment, whip the butter on medium-high speed for 5 minutes, or until pale and creamy. Add the powdered sugar and mix on low speed until fully incorporated. Add the vanilla, cotton candy extract and salt. Slowly drizzle in the heavy cream. Turn the mixer to medium speed and whip the buttercream for 2 to 3 minutes, or until smooth and creamy. Divide the buttercream in half. Tint one portion of the frosting pink and the other portion light blue with gel food coloring.

ASSEMBLING THE CUPCAKES

Fill a piping bag fitted with a Wilton 1M piping tip with the cotton candy buttercream. Add the pink to one side of the piping bag and blue on the other side to create a color swirl. Pipe an "ice cream swirl" (see page 15 for more instructions) of buttercream on the cupcakes. Immediately before serving, sprinkle with the cotton candy popping candies and add puffs of cotton candy to each cupcake.

FEELING KINDA NUTTY CUPCAKES

SONG: Whitney Houston—I Wanna Dance With Somebody (1987)

YIELD: 12 cupcakes

Don'tcha wanna bake, say you wanna bake, don'tcha wanna bake these chocolate almond coconut cupcakes? When you feel like a nut, just bake your blues away with this recipe. These decadent chocolate treats are frosted with creamy coconut buttercream frosting, rolled in toasted coconut and topped with chocolate ganache and roasted almonds. If you are an Almond Joy™ fan, this recipe will have you singing, "I wanna bake with somebody, I wanna feel the heat of my oven."

CHOCOLATE ALMOND CUPCAKES

¾ cup (180 ml) boiling water

¼ cup (42 g) semisweet or dark chocolate chips

¼ cup (25 g) dark cocoa powder

¾ cup (94 g) all-purpose flour

¾ cup (150 g) granulated sugar

½ tsp baking soda

½ tsp salt

⅓ cup (80 ml) vegetable oil

2 large eggs, at room temperature

1 tsp vanilla extract

¼ cup (35 g) finely chopped roasted almonds

COCONUT BUTTERCREAM FROSTING

1 cup (227 g/2 sticks) unsalted butter, at room temperature

2½ (300 g) cups powdered sugar

2 tsp (10 ml) coconut extract

1 tsp vanilla extract

¼ tsp salt

2 tbsp (30 ml) heavy cream

ADDITIONAL INGREDIENTS

1 cup (70 g) toasted sweetened shredded coconut

1 batch Most Excellent Chocolate Ganache Drizzle (page 143)

12 roasted almonds

CHOCOLATE ALMOND CUPCAKES

Preheat the oven to 350°F (177°C). Prepare a cupcake pan with 12 cupcake liners.

In a medium-sized bowl, stir together the boiling water, chocolate chips and dark cocoa powder until the chocolate chips are melted. Set aside to cool for 5 minutes.

In a large bowl, whisk together the flour, granulated sugar, baking soda and salt. Pour in the cooled chocolate mixture and whisk until well combined. Add the vegetable oil, eggs and vanilla, and whisk until combined and smooth.

Pour the cupcake batter into the cupcake liners about two-thirds full. Sprinkle the finely chopped almonds over the cupcake batter. Bake the cupcakes for 20 minutes, or until their tops bounce back when gently touched. Remove them from the oven and let the cupcakes cool in the pan for 5 minutes, then transfer to a wire rack to cool completely.

COCONUT BUTTERCREAM FROSTING

In the bowl of a stand mixer fitted with a paddle attachment, whip the butter on medium-high speed for 5 minutes, or until pale and creamy. Add the powdered sugar and mix on low speed until fully incorporated with the butter. Add the coconut extract, vanilla and salt. Slowly drizzle in the heavy cream. Scrape the sides and bottom of the bowl as needed. Turn the mixer to medium speed and whip the buttercream for 2 to 3 minutes, or until smooth and creamy.

ASSEMBLING THE CUPCAKES

Fill a piping bag fitted with a Wilton 1A piping tip with the coconut buttercream. Pipe an "ice cream swirl" (see page 15 for more instructions) of frosting onto the cupcakes. Gently press the frosted cupcakes into the toasted coconut, covering the entire buttercream swirl. Drizzle chocolate ganache onto the cupcakes and add an almond to the top.

92 GIRLS JUST WANNA BAKE CUPCAKES

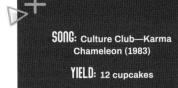

SONG: Culture Club—Karma Chameleon (1983)

YIELD: 12 cupcakes

KARMA CANDYLAND CUPCAKES

These "karma karma karma karma karma" Candyland cupcakes will come and go as fast as you can bake them. They start off with colorful confetti cake swirled with creamy meringue buttercream frosting. Before you find King Kandy, make a stop in the Candy Cane Forest to gather up some sweet treats to decorate them. Use your favorite candies, but might I suggest lollipops that are red, gold and green? If you think your love is an addiction, wait until you tumble for these cupcakes. When they go, they're gone forever, at least until you bake up another batch.

CONFETTI CUPCAKES

1¼ cups (156 g) all-purpose flour

1½ tsp (7 g) baking powder

½ tsp salt

¾ cup (150 g) granulated sugar

¼ cup (57 g/½ stick) unsalted butter, at room temperature

¼ cup (60 ml) vegetable oil

2 large egg whites, at room temperature

2 tbsp (30 ml) sour cream, at room temperature

2 tsp (10 ml) vanilla extract

½ cup (120 ml) milk, at room temperature

¼ cup (45 g) rainbow sprinkles

MERINGUE BUTTERCREAM FROSTING

3 oz (90 ml) pasteurized egg whites (from a carton), at room temperature

2½ cups (300 g) powdered sugar

2 tsp (10 ml) vanilla extract

¼ tsp salt

1 cup (227 g/2 sticks) unsalted butter, at room temperature

2 to 3 drops sky blue gel food coloring

ADDITIONAL INGREDIENTS

Assorted colorful candies

CONFETTI CUPCAKES

Preheat the oven to 350°F (177°C). Prepare a cupcake pan with 12 cupcake liners.

In a medium-sized bowl, whisk together the flour, baking powder and salt. Set aside.

In a large bowl, use an electric hand mixer to cream together the granulated sugar, butter and vegetable oil until pale and creamy. Add the egg whites, sour cream and vanilla. Mix on medium speed until smooth. Add half of the flour mixture to the batter and mix on low speed until mostly combined. Slowly pour in the milk while continuing to mix on low speed. Add the remaining flour mixture and mix until combined and smooth. Fold in the rainbow sprinkles.

Portion the cupcake batter into the cupcake liners about three-quarters full. Bake the cupcakes for 20 minutes, or until their tops bounce back when gently touched. Remove them from the oven and let the cupcakes cool in the pan for 5 minutes, then transfer to a wire rack to cool completely.

MERINGUE BUTTERCREAM FROSTING

In the bowl of a stand mixer fitted with a whisk attachment, whip the egg whites and powdered sugar on medium-high speed for 5 to 10 minutes, or until thick and opaque. Add the vanilla and salt. Turn the mixer to low speed and add the softened butter, 1 tablespoon (14 g) at a time, mixing in between each addition. Add a few drops of the gel food coloring. Turn the mixer to medium-high speed and whip the frosting, scraping the bowl occasionally, for 10 to 15 minutes, or until smooth and creamy.

ASSEMBLING THE CUPCAKES

Fill a piping bag fitted with a Wilton 2D piping tip with the meringue buttercream frosting. Pipe a "ruffle swirl" (see page 15 for more instructions) of buttercream onto the cupcakes. Decorate the cupcakes with assorted colorful candies.

'80S MOVIE NIGHT CUPCAKES

SONG: Def Leppard—Pour Some Sugar on Me (1987)

YIELD: 12 cupcakes

Do you take sugar? One cupcake or two? The best movies are '80s movies, and these movie night cupcakes are the perfect snack for '80s movie marathons. Whether you are a *Fast Times at Ridgemont High*, *The Goonies* or *Top Gun* fan, these cupcakes will *sometime*, anytime sugar you sweet. They are made with red velvet cake swirled with chocolate cream cheese frosting and piled high with your favorite movie theater candies. Choose your favorite hot, sticky sweets to pour some sugar on these cupcakes. All I know is, I can't get enough.

RED VELVET CUPCAKES

1¼ cups (156 g) all-purpose flour

1 tbsp (5 g) unsweetened cocoa powder

¾ tsp baking soda

½ tsp salt

¾ cup (150 g) granulated sugar

½ cup (120 ml) vegetable oil

1 large egg, at room temperature

2 tsp (10 ml) vanilla extract

½ tsp white vinegar

1 tsp red gel food coloring

½ cup (120 ml) buttermilk, at room temperature

CHOCOLATE CREAM CHEESE FROSTING

¾ cup (170 g/1½ sticks) unsalted butter, at room temperature

4 oz (113 g) cream cheese, at room temperature

2½ cups (300 g) powdered sugar

¼ cup (25 g) dark cocoa powder

2 tsp (10 ml) vanilla extract

¼ tsp salt

1 tbsp (15 ml) heavy cream

ADDITIONAL INGREDIENTS

Assorted movie theater candies

RED VELVET CUPCAKES

Preheat the oven to 350°F (177°C). Prepare a cupcake pan with 12 cupcake liners.

In a medium-sized bowl, whisk together the flour, cocoa powder, baking soda and salt. Set aside.

In a large bowl, use an electric hand mixer to mix the granulated sugar, vegetable oil, egg, vanilla, white vinegar and red gel food coloring until well combined. Add half of the flour mixture to the red mixture and mix on low speed until well incorporated. Slowly pour in the buttermilk while mixing on low speed. Add the remaining flour mixture and mix until the red velvet batter is smooth.

Portion the cupcake batter into the cupcake liners about three-quarters full. Bake the cupcakes for 20 minutes, or until their tops spring back when gently touched. Remove them from the oven and let the cupcakes cool in the pan for 5 minutes, then transfer to a wire rack to cool to room temperature.

CHOCOLATE CREAM CHEESE FROSTING

In the bowl of a stand mixer fitted with a whisk attachment, whip the butter and cream cheese on medium-high speed until light, fluffy and smooth. Add the powdered sugar, dark cocoa powder, vanilla and salt. Mix on low speed until all the ingredients are well combined. Scrape the sides and bottom of the bowl as needed. On low speed, drizzle in the heavy cream. Turn the mixer to medium-high speed and whip the frosting for an additional 2 to 3 minutes, or until smooth and creamy.

ASSEMBLING THE CUPCAKES

Fill a piping bag fitted with an Ateco 826 piping tip with the chocolate cream cheese frosting. Pipe a "double swirl" (see page 13 for more instructions) of frosting onto the cupcakes. Decorate with your favorite movie theater candies.

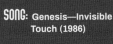

SONG: Genesis—Invisible Touch (1986)

YIELD: 12 cupcakes

FANCY-SCHMANCY CHOCOLATE HAZELNUT CUPCAKES

I've been waiting, waiting here so long, to share this truly decadent recipe. Trust me, these cupcakes will mess up your life, but you'll want them just the same. The moist and fudgy chocolate cake is filled with creamy chocolate hazelnut spread, frosted with chocolate hazelnut buttercream frosting, drizzled with even more chocolate hazelnut spread and topped with a very classy and sophisticated chocolate hazelnut candy. These will reach in and grab right hold of your heart.

CHOCOLATE CUPCAKES

¾ cup (180 ml) boiling water

¼ cup (42 g) semisweet or dark chocolate chips

¼ cup (25 g) dark cocoa powder

1 tsp instant espresso powder

¾ cup (94 g) all-purpose flour

¾ cup (150 g) granulated sugar

½ tsp baking soda

½ tsp salt

⅓ cup (80 ml) vegetable oil

2 large eggs, at room temperature

1 tsp vanilla extract

CHOCOLATE HAZELNUT BUTTERCREAM FROSTING

1 cup (227 g/2 sticks) unsalted butter, at room temperature

2½ cups (300 g) powdered sugar

½ cup (150 g) chocolate hazelnut spread (I prefer Nutella® brand)

1 tsp vanilla extract

¼ tsp salt

2 tbsp (30 ml) heavy cream

ADDITIONAL INGREDIENTS

½ cup (150 g) + 2 tbsp (37 g) chocolate hazelnut spread, divided

12 chocolate hazelnut candies (I prefer Ferrero Rocher® brand)

4 chocolate hazelnut wafer cookies, cut into thirds

CHOCOLATE CUPCAKES

Preheat the oven to 350°F (177°C). Prepare a cupcake pan with 12 cupcake liners.

In a medium-sized bowl, stir together the boiling water, chocolate chips, dark cocoa powder and instant espresso powder until the chocolate chips are melted. Set aside to cool for 5 minutes.

In a large bowl, whisk together the flour, granulated sugar, baking soda and salt. Pour in the cooled chocolate mixture and whisk until well combined. Add the vegetable oil, eggs and vanilla, and whisk until the batter is smooth.

Pour the cupcake batter into the cupcake liners about two-thirds full. Bake the cupcakes for 20 minutes, or until they spring back when gently touched. Remove them from the oven and let the cupcakes cool in the pan for 5 minutes, then transfer to a wire rack to cool completely.

CHOCOLATE HAZELNUT BUTTERCREAM FROSTING

In the bowl of a stand mixer fitted with a paddle attachment, whip the butter on medium-high speed for 5 minutes, or until pale and creamy. Add the powdered sugar and mix on low speed until fully incorporated with the butter. Add the chocolate hazelnut spread, vanilla and salt. Slowly drizzle in the heavy cream until fully incorporated. Scrape the sides and bottom of the bowl as needed. Turn the mixer to medium speed and whip the buttercream for 2 to 3 minutes, or until smooth and creamy.

ASSEMBLING THE CUPCAKES

Core the cupcakes to remove the center. Use a piping bag with the tip cut off to fill the cupcakes with the ½ cup (150 g) of chocolate hazelnut spread. Fill a piping bag fitted with a Wilton 1M piping tip with the buttercream. Pipe an "ice cream swirl" (see page 15 for more instructions) of the frosting onto the cupcakes. In a microwave-safe bowl, heat the 2 tablespoons (37 g) of chocolate hazelnut spread in a microwave for 15 seconds to melt. Drizzle the melted spread over the cupcakes and add a chocolate hazelnut candy and a chocolate hazelnut wafer cookie piece to each cupcake.

SUMMER OF '89

Life is just a party and parties weren't meant to last, and neither will these cupcakes. Cupcakes are the perfect celebratory treat and there is no better way to party like it's 1989 than with these summer-inspired cupcake flavors. These recipes are fresh, fruity and colorful, kind of like the '80s. So, if you are spending the summer at Kellerman's, heading across the country to Walley World or working at a beachside bar in Jamaica, these summer cupcakes will help you make lots of friends.

In this chapter, we will cool things down with refreshing summer drink flavors like raspberry lemonade (page 104), cherry limeade (page 111) and the infamous piña colada (page 115). Let's celebrate the fruits of summer with a triple berry cupcake (page 112), lemon blueberry cupcake (page 116) and blackberry peach cupcake (page 107). These bright, fruity flavors will add some zing to any cruel, cruel summer and just may make your dreams come true. So, if you want to cut loose, footloose in Kokomo, bake these cupcakes and the summer will seem to last forever. After the boys of summer have gone, the girls will still just wanna bake cupcakes.

SONG: Hall and Oates—You Make
My Dreams Come True (1981)

YIELD: 12 cupcakes

AWESOME ICE CREAM CONE CUPCAKES

These cupcakes will make your dreams come true. You'll be waking up to fantasies of childhood birthdays covered in rainbow sprinkles. Broken ice still melts in the sun, but these treats sure won't. Here, colorful confetti cake is baked into an ice cream cone, swirled with smooth and creamy vanilla buttercream frosting and covered with rainbow sprinkles. These ice cream cone cupcakes will convert any man-eater into a cupcake-eater. Put this recipe on your list because it's one of the best things in life.

CONFETTI ICE CREAM CONE CUPCAKES

12 jumbo cake ice cream cones

1¼ cups (156 g) all-purpose flour

1½ tsp (7 g) baking powder

½ tsp salt

¾ cup (150 g) granulated sugar

¼ cup (57 g/½ stick) unsalted butter, at room temperature

¼ cup (60 ml) vegetable oil

2 large egg whites, at room temperature

2 tbsp (30 ml) sour cream, at room temperature

2 tsp (10 ml) vanilla extract

½ tsp almond extract

⅓ cup (80 ml) milk, at room temperature

¼ cup (45 g) rainbow sprinkles

VANILLA BUTTERCREAM FROSTING

1½ cups (340 g/3 sticks) unsalted butter, at room temperature

3½ cups (420 g) powdered sugar

1 tbsp (15 ml) vanilla extract

½ tsp salt

3 tbsp (45 ml) heavy cream

2 to 3 drops pink gel food coloring

ADDITIONAL INGREDIENTS

2 tbsp (30 g) rainbow nonpareil sprinkles

CONFETTI ICE CREAM CONE CUPCAKES

Move the oven rack to a lower position and preheat the oven to 350°F (177°C). Cover a cupcake pan with aluminum foil and cut an X-shaped slit into the aluminum foil in the center of each cup. Insert an ice cream cone in each slit (12 ice cream cones total).

In a medium-sized bowl, whisk together the flour, baking powder and salt. Set aside.

In a large bowl, use an electric hand mixer to cream the granulated sugar, butter and vegetable oil until light and fluffy. Add the egg whites, sour cream, vanilla and almond extract, and mix on medium speed until smooth. Add half of the flour mixture to the batter and mix on low speed until mostly combined. Slowly pour in the milk while mixing on low speed. Add the remaining flour mixture and mix until combined and smooth. Fold in the rainbow sprinkles.

Portion the cupcake batter into the ice cream cones, about 3 tablespoons (45 ml) of batter in each cone. Bake the cupcakes for 25 to 30 minutes, or until their tops bounce back when gently touched. Remove them from the oven and let the cupcakes cool in the pan.

VANILLA BUTTERCREAM FROSTING

In the bowl of a stand mixer fitted with a paddle attachment, whip the butter on medium-high speed for 5 minutes, or until pale and creamy. Add the powdered sugar and mix on low speed until fully incorporated. Add the vanilla and salt. Slowly drizzle in the heavy cream and add a few drops of gel food coloring. Scrape the sides and bottom of the bowl as needed. Turn the mixer to medium speed and whip the buttercream for 2 to 3 minutes, or until smooth and creamy.

ASSEMBLING THE CUPCAKES

The easiest way to frost the cupcakes is to keep them in the cupcake pan. Fill a piping bag fitted with an Ateco 826 piping tip with the vanilla buttercream. Pipe an "ice cream swirl"—obviously!—of frosting (see page 15 for more instructions). Sprinkle the cupcakes with nonpareil rainbow sprinkles.

ROCKIN' RASPBERRY LEMONADE CUPCAKES

SONG: Lindsey Buckingham— Holiday Road (1983)

YIELD: 12 cupcakes

I found out long ago it's a long way down the holiday road, so you better bring snacks. Might I suggest a tall, cold glass of raspberry lemonade, but make it a cupcake? There is no better treat to haul across the country to Walley World than these cupcakes. They are made with light and fluffy lemon cake, and raspberry buttercream frosting adds bright, fresh and fruity raspberry flavor. These cupcakes will cool you down quicker than taking a dip in a motel pool.

LEMON CUPCAKES
1¼ cups (156 g) all-purpose flour

1½ tsp (7 g) baking powder

½ tsp salt

¾ cup (150 g) granulated sugar

¼ cup (57 g/½ stick) unsalted butter, at room temperature

¼ cup (60 ml) vegetable oil

1 large egg, at room temperature

2 tbsp (30 ml) sour cream, at room temperature

1 tsp lemon zest

¼ cup (60 ml) fresh lemon juice

¼ cup (60 ml) milk, at room temperature

RASPBERRY BUTTERCREAM FROSTING
1 cup (227 g/2 sticks) unsalted butter, at room temperature

2½ cups (300 g) powdered sugar

¼ cup (60 ml) raspberry Berrylicious Berry Reduction (page 151)

1 tsp vanilla extract

¼ tsp salt

1 tbsp (15 ml) heavy cream

ADDITIONAL INGREDIENTS
12 lemon slices

12 fresh raspberries

LEMON CUPCAKES
Preheat the oven to 350°F (177°C). Line a cupcake pan with 12 cupcake liners.

In a medium-sized bowl, whisk together the flour, baking powder and salt. Set aside.

In a large bowl, cream the granulated sugar, butter and vegetable oil with an electric mixer for a few minutes until light, pale and smooth. Add the egg, sour cream and lemon zest, and mix on medium speed until well combined. Add half of the flour mixture to the batter and mix on low speed until incorporated. Slowly pour in the lemon juice and milk while mixing on low speed. Add the remaining flour mixture and mix until combined and smooth.

Portion the cupcake batter into the cupcake liners about three-quarters full. Bake the cupcakes for 20 minutes, or until their tops bounce back when gently touched. Remove them from the oven and let the cupcakes cool in the pan for 5 minutes, then transfer to a wire rack to cool completely.

RASPBERRY BUTTERCREAM FROSTING
In the bowl of a stand mixer fitted with a paddle attachment, whip the butter on medium-high speed for 5 minutes, or until pale and creamy. Add the powdered sugar and mix on low speed until fully incorporated with the butter. Add the raspberry reduction, vanilla and salt. Slowly drizzle in the heavy cream until fully incorporated. Scrape the sides and bottom of the bowl as needed. Turn the mixer to medium speed and whip the buttercream for 3 to 5 minutes, or until smooth and creamy.

ASSEMBLING THE CUPCAKES
Fill a piping bag fitted with a Wilton 1M piping tip with the raspberry buttercream frosting. Pipe an "ice cream swirl" (see page 15 for more instructions) of buttercream onto the cupcakes. Add fresh lemon slices and raspberries to decorate the cupcakes.

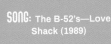

SONG: The B-52's—Love Shack (1989)

YIELD: 12 cupcakes

BANG BANG BANG
BLACKBERRY PEACH CUPCAKES

Move over orange Popsicles® and lemonade. This summer of love we are trying something different. If you are heading down to the love shack, be sure to bring these cupcakes, because folks will be lining up outside just to get one. They are a fluffy vanilla cake packed with peaches and blackberries, frosted with sweet blackberry buttercream frosting and topped with fresh peach slices and blackberries. Since there is already glitter on the mattress, highway, front porch and hallway, why not add a little sprinkle of edible glitter on these cupcakes?

BLACKBERRY PEACH CUPCAKES

1¼ cups (156 g) all-purpose flour

1½ tsp (7 g) baking powder

½ tsp salt

¾ cup (150 g) granulated sugar

¼ cup (57 g/½ stick) unsalted butter, at room temperature

¼ cup (60 ml) vegetable oil

1 large egg, at room temperature

2 tbsp (30 ml) sour cream, at room temperature

2 tsp (10 ml) vanilla extract

⅓ cup (80 ml) milk, at room temperature

⅓ cup (55 g) finely diced fresh peach

⅓ cup (50 g) finely diced fresh blackberries

BLACKBERRY BUTTERCREAM FROSTING

1 cup (227 g/2 sticks) unsalted butter, at room temperature

2½ cups (300 g) powdered sugar

¼ cup (60 ml) blackberry Berrylicious Berry Reduction (page 151)

1 tsp vanilla extract

¼ tsp salt

1 tbsp (15 ml) heavy cream

ADDITIONAL INGREDIENTS

12 blackberries

12 peach slices

Edible glitter

BLACKBERRY PEACH CUPCAKES

Preheat the oven to 350°F (177°C). Line a cupcake pan with 12 cupcake liners.

In a medium-sized bowl, whisk together the flour, baking powder and salt. Set aside.

In a large bowl, use an electric mixer to cream the granulated sugar, butter and vegetable oil for a few minutes, or until pale and creamy. Add the egg, sour cream and vanilla, and mix until smooth. Add half of the flour mixture to the batter and mix on low speed until incorporated. Slowly pour in the milk while mixing on low speed. Add the remaining flour mixture and mix until the batter is smooth. Fold in the diced peaches and blackberries.

Portion the cupcake batter into the cupcake liners about three-quarters full. Bake the cupcakes for 20 minutes, or until their tops bounce back when gently touched. Remove them from the oven and let the cupcakes cool in the pan for 5 minutes, then transfer to a wire rack to cool completely.

BLACKBERRY BUTTERCREAM FROSTING

In the bowl of a stand mixer fitted with a paddle attachment, whip the butter on medium-high speed for 5 minutes, or until pale and creamy. Add the powdered sugar and mix on low speed until fully incorporated. Add the blackberry reduction, vanilla and salt. Slowly drizzle in the heavy cream until fully incorporated. Scrape the sides and bottom of the bowl as needed. Turn the mixer to medium speed and whip the buttercream for 3 to 5 minutes, or until smooth and creamy.

ASSEMBLING THE CUPCAKES

Fill a piping bag fitted with an Ateco 826 piping tip with the blackberry buttercream frosting. Pipe an "ice cream swirl" (see page 15 for more instructions) of the frosting onto the cupcakes. Add a fresh blackberry and peach slice to the top of each cupcake and sprinkle with edible glitter.

BANANARAMA SPLIT CUPCAKES

SONG: Bananarama—Cruel Summer (1984)

YIELD: 12 to 14 cupcakes

Hot summer streets and the pavements are burning, but let's cool things down with a banana split. Nothing says it's a cruel, cruel summer like an unmeltable sundae. The cupcakes are made with banana cake, homemade strawberry filling and Swiss meringue buttercream that tastes just like vanilla ice cream. Drizzle with some chocolate ganache, add rainbow sprinkles and then put the cherry on the sundae. I don't know about you, but I'm guilty of love in the first degree with this scrumptious recipe.

BANANA CUPCAKES

1¼ cups (156 g) all-purpose flour

1½ tsp (7 g) baking powder

½ tsp salt

¾ cup (150 g) granulated sugar

¼ cup (57 g/½ stick) unsalted butter, at room temperature

¼ cup (60 ml) vegetable oil

⅔ cup (180 g) mashed ripe banana

2 tbsp (30 ml) sour cream, at room temperature

1 large egg, at room temperature

2 tsp (10 ml) vanilla extract

⅓ cup (80 ml) milk, at room temperature

VANILLA SWISS MERINGUE BUTTERCREAM FROSTING

3 large egg whites, at room temperature

½ cup (100 g) granulated sugar

¼ tsp salt

1¼ cups (284 g) unsalted butter, at room temperature

2 tsp (10 ml) vanilla extract

ADDITIONAL INGREDIENTS

1 batch strawberry Funky Fresh Fruit Filling (page 148)

2 batches Most Excellent Chocolate Ganache Drizzle (page 143)

1 tbsp (15 g) rainbow nonpareil sprinkles

12 to 14 maraschino cherries

BANANA CUPCAKES

Preheat the oven to 350°F (177°C). Line two cupcake pans with 12 to 14 cupcake liners.

In a medium-sized bowl, whisk together the flour, baking powder and salt. Set aside.

In a large bowl, use an electric hand mixer to cream together the granulated sugar, butter and vegetable oil until smooth. Add the mashed banana, sour cream, egg and vanilla, and mix well. Add half of the flour mixture and mix on low speed until incorporated. Slowly pour in the milk, add the remaining flour mixture and mix until the batter is smooth.

Portion the cupcake batter into the cupcake liners about three-quarters full. Bake the cupcakes for 20 minutes, or until their tops bounce back when gently touched. Remove them from the oven and let the cupcakes cool in the pans for 5 minutes, then transfer to a wire rack to cool completely.

VANILLA SWISS MERINGUE BUTTERCREAM FROSTING

In a heatproof bowl over a pot of simmering water on the stovetop, whisk together the egg whites, granulated sugar and salt. Gently heat the mixture, stirring constantly, until the sugar granules dissolve. Transfer the egg white mixture to the bowl of a stand mixer fitted with a whisk attachment. Whip the egg whites on medium-high speed until glossy, stiff peaks form. Turn the mixer to low speed and add the room temperature butter, 1 tablespoon (14 g) at a time. Add the vanilla. Turn the mixer to medium-high speed and whip the buttercream for 5 to 10 minutes, or until smooth and creamy.

ASSEMBLING THE CUPCAKES

Core the cupcakes to remove the center. Use a piping bag with the tip cut off to fill the cupcakes with the strawberry filling. Fill a piping bag fitted with a Wilton 2D piping tip with the buttercream. Pipe a "ruffle swirl" (see page 15 for more instructions) of frosting onto the cupcakes. Decorate the cupcakes with chocolate ganache, rainbow sprinkles and maraschino cherries.

SHAKE YOUR CHERRY LIMEADE CUPCAKES

Everybody gather 'round now for this too hot-to-handle recipe. Feel the fire of desire with these cherry limeade cupcakes, made with cherry cake and like sugarcane, so sweet, frosted in a tangy lime buttercream frosting. Top them with slices of lime and maraschino cherries (don't fight it 'til you've tried it). I know you can't control yourself any longer around these treats, so make two batches to be safe.

CHERRY CUPCAKES

1¼ cups (156 g) all-purpose flour

1½ tsp (7 g) baking powder

½ tsp salt

¾ cup (150 g) granulated sugar

¼ cup (57 g/½ stick) unsalted butter, at room temperature

¼ cup (60 ml) vegetable oil

2 large egg whites, at room temperature

2 tbsp (30 ml) sour cream, at room temperature

1 tsp vanilla extract

Drop of red gel food coloring

6 tbsp (90 ml) milk, at room temperature

2 tbsp (30 ml) maraschino cherry juice

½ cup (100 g) chopped maraschino cherries

LIME BUTTERCREAM FROSTING

1 cup (227 g/2 sticks) unsalted butter, at room temperature

2½ cups (300 g) powdered sugar

½ tsp lime zest

¼ tsp salt

2 tbsp (30 ml) fresh lime juice

1 tbsp (15 ml) heavy cream

1 to 2 drops each yellow and green gel food coloring (optional)

ADDITIONAL INGREDIENTS

12 lime slices

12 maraschino cherries

CHERRY CUPCAKES

Preheat the oven to 350°F (177°C). Line a cupcake pan with 12 cupcake liners.

In a medium-sized bowl, whisk together the flour, baking powder and salt. Set aside.

In a large bowl, cream together the granulated sugar, butter and vegetable oil with an electric mixer until light, pale and smooth. Add the egg whites, sour cream, vanilla and red gel food coloring and mix on medium speed until smooth. Add half of the flour mixture and mix on low speed until incorporated. Slowly pour in the milk and maraschino cherry juice, continuing to mix on low speed. Add the remaining flour mixture and mix until the batter is smooth. Fold in the chopped maraschino cherries.

Portion the cupcake batter into the cupcake liners about three-quarters full. Bake the cupcakes for 20 minutes, or until their tops bounce back when gently touched. Remove them from the oven and let the cupcakes cool in the pan for 5 minutes, then transfer to a wire rack to cool completely.

LIME BUTTERCREAM FROSTING

In the bowl of a stand mixer fitted with a paddle attachment, whip the butter on medium-high speed for 5 minutes, or until pale and creamy. Add the powdered sugar and mix on low speed until fully incorporated with the butter. Add the lime zest and salt. Drizzle in the lime juice and heavy cream, and add one or two drops each of yellow and green gel food coloring, if desired. Turn the mixer to medium speed and whip the buttercream for 2 to 3 minutes, or until smooth and creamy.

ASSEMBLING THE CUPCAKES

Fill a piping bag fitted with a Wilton 1M piping tip with the lime buttercream frosting. Pipe an "ice cream swirl" (see page 15 for more instructions) of frosting onto the cupcakes. Decorate the cupcakes with slices of lime and maraschino cherries.

LOSE YOUR BLUES TRIPLE BERRY CUPCAKES

SONG: Kenny Loggins—Footloose (1984)

YIELD: 12 cupcakes

Been working so hard, so you deserve a special treat. These triple-threat treats will help you lose your blues and cut footloose. And while you are baking, turn up the tunes and break the antidancing ordinance in your kitchen (I won't tell). The cupcakes are made of a tender vanilla cake studded with fresh chopped raspberries, blueberries and blackberries. Then, they are generously swirled with a triple berry buttercream frosting and topped with even more berries. How could we ask for more?

TRIPLE BERRY CUPCAKES

1¼ cups (156 g) all-purpose flour

1½ tsp (7 g) baking powder

½ tsp salt

¾ cup (150 g) granulated sugar

¼ cup (57 g/½ stick) unsalted butter, at room temperature

¼ cup (60 ml) vegetable oil

1 large egg, at room temperature

2 tbsp (30 ml) sour cream, at room temperature

2 tsp (10 ml) vanilla extract

⅓ cup (80 ml) milk, at room temperature

¼ cup (40 g) chopped fresh raspberries

¼ cup (40 g) chopped fresh blueberries

¼ cup (40 g) chopped fresh blackberries

TRIPLE BERRY BUTTERCREAM FROSTING

1 cup (227 g/2 sticks) unsalted butter, at room temperature

2½ cups (300 g) powdered sugar

¼ cup (60 ml) triple berry Berrylicious Berry Reduction (page 151)

1 tsp vanilla extract

¼ tsp salt

1 tbsp (15 ml) heavy cream

ADDITIONAL INGREDIENTS

Fresh raspberries, blueberries and blackberries

TRIPLE BERRY CUPCAKES

Preheat the oven to 350°F (177°C). Line a cupcake pan with 12 cupcake liners.

In a medium-sized bowl, whisk together the flour, baking powder and salt. Set aside.

In a large bowl, use an electric hand mixer to cream together the granulated sugar, butter and vegetable oil for a few minutes, or until pale and creamy. Add the egg, sour cream and vanilla, and mix on medium speed until well combined. Add half of the flour mixture to the batter and mix on low speed until incorporated. Slowly pour in the milk while mixing on low speed. Add the remaining flour mixture and mix until smooth. Gently fold in the raspberries, blueberries and blackberries.

Portion the cupcake batter into the cupcake liners about three-quarters full. Bake the cupcakes for 20 minutes, or until their tops bounce back when gently touched. Remove them from the oven and let the cupcakes cool in the pan for 5 minutes, then transfer to a wire rack to cool completely.

TRIPLE BERRY BUTTERCREAM FROSTING

In the bowl of a stand mixer fitted with a paddle attachment, whip the butter on medium-high speed for 5 minutes, or until pale and creamy. Add the powdered sugar and mix on low speed until fully incorporated with the butter. Add the triple berry reduction, vanilla and salt. Slowly drizzle in the heavy cream. Scrape the sides and bottom of the bowl as needed. Turn the mixer to medium speed and whip the buttercream for 3 to 5 minutes, or until smooth and creamy.

ASSEMBLING THE CUPCAKES

Fill a piping bag fitted with an Ateco 857 piping tip with the triple berry buttercream. Pipe an "ice cream swirl" (see page 15 for more instructions) of frosting onto the cupcakes and garnish the cupcakes with fresh raspberries, blueberries and blackberries.

IF YOU LIKE PIÑA COLADA CUPCAKES

You don't have to go to Aruba, Jamaica, Bermuda, Bahama, Key Largo, Montego or even Kokomo to get a taste of the tropics. Rather than having a tropical drink melting in your hand, let's turn this classic cocktail flavor into an irresistible dessert. The cupcakes are made with tender pineapple cake and frosted with creamy coconut buttercream. Top with toasted coconut, pineapple, maraschino cherries and of course, cocktail umbrellas for a little tropical contact high. Enjoy these from the comfort of your own home until the time comes for your next tropical vacation.

PINEAPPLE CUPCAKES

1¼ cups (156 g) all-purpose flour

1½ tsp (7 g) baking powder

½ tsp salt

¾ cup (150 g) granulated sugar

¼ cup (57 g/½ stick) unsalted butter, at room temperature

¼ cup (60 ml) vegetable oil

1 large egg, at room temperature

½ cup (140 g) crushed pineapple, undrained

2 tbsp (30 ml) sour cream, at room temperature

2 tsp (10 ml) vanilla extract

¼ cup (60 ml) pineapple juice, at room temperature

COCONUT BUTTERCREAM FROSTING

1 cup (227 g/2 sticks) unsalted butter, at room temperature

2½ cups (300 g) powdered sugar

1½ tsp (8 ml) coconut extract

1 tsp vanilla extract

¼ tsp salt

2 tbsp (30 ml) heavy cream

ADDITIONAL INGREDIENTS

12 pineapple slices

¼ cup (20 g) toasted sweetened shredded coconut

12 maraschino cherries

PINEAPPLE CUPCAKES

Preheat the oven to 350°F (177°C). Line a cupcake pan with 12 cupcake liners.

In a medium-sized bowl, whisk together the flour, baking powder and salt. Set aside.

In a large bowl, use an electric hand mixer to cream together the granulated sugar, butter and vegetable oil for a few minutes, or until pale and creamy. Add the egg, crushed pineapple, sour cream and vanilla, and mix until well combined. Add half of the flour mixture to the batter and mix on low speed until incorporated. Slowly pour in the pineapple juice while mixing on low speed. Add the remaining flour mixture and mix until the batter is well combined.

Portion the cupcake batter into the cupcake liners about three-quarters full. Bake the cupcakes for 20 minutes, or until their tops bounce back when gently touched. Remove them from the oven and let the cupcakes cool in the pan for 5 minutes, then transfer to a wire rack to cool completely.

COCONUT BUTTERCREAM FROSTING

In the bowl of a stand mixer fitted with a paddle attachment, whip the butter on medium-high speed for 5 minutes, or until pale and creamy. Add the powdered sugar and mix on low speed until fully incorporated. Add the coconut extract, vanilla and salt. Drizzle in the heavy cream. Turn the mixer to medium speed and whip the buttercream for 2 to 3 minutes, or until smooth and creamy.

ASSEMBLING THE CUPCAKES

Fill a piping bag fitted with an Ateco 869 piping tip with the coconut buttercream. Pipe an "ice cream swirl" (see page 15 for more instructions) of frosting onto the cupcakes, twisting the piping tip slightly. Decorate the cupcakes with pineapple slices, toasted coconut and maraschino cherries. Add a cocktail umbrella for extra tropical vibes.

LIVIN' ON LEMON BLUEBERRY CUPCAKES

SONG: Cyndi Lauper—Girls Just Want to Have Fun (1983)

YIELD: 12 cupcakes

Lying in my bed, I hear the clock tick and think of these cupcakes. They are so delectable, you will want to bake them time after time. These summery fruit flavors combined into one adorable little cupcake? Um, yes please! And let's face it, girls just wanna bake cupcakes! They are made with tart lemon cake flavored with lemon juice and zest and studded with fresh blueberries. The perfect complement to the cake is a sweet and tangy lemon cream cheese frosting topped with lemon rind curls and fresh blueberries. That's good enough for me.

LEMON BLUEBERRY CUPCAKES
1¼ cups (156 g) all-purpose flour

1½ tsp (7 g) baking powder

½ tsp salt

¾ cup (150 g) granulated sugar

¼ cup (57 g/½ stick) unsalted butter, at room temperature

¼ cup (60 ml) vegetable oil

1 large egg, at room temperature

2 tbsp (30 ml) sour cream, at room temperature

1 tsp lemon zest

¼ cup (60 ml) fresh lemon juice

¼ cup (60 ml) milk, at room temperature

½ cup (75 g) blueberries (small blueberries work best)

LEMON CREAM CHEESE FROSTING
¾ cup (170 g/1½ sticks) unsalted butter, at room temperature

4 oz (113 g) cream cheese, at room temperature

2½ cups (300 g) powdered sugar

1 tsp lemon zest

¼ tsp salt

2 tbsp (30 ml) fresh lemon juice

ADDITIONAL INGREDIENTS
36 fresh blueberries

12 lemon rind curls

LEMON BLUEBERRY CUPCAKES
Preheat the oven to 350°F (177°C). Line a cupcake pan with 12 cupcake liners.

In a medium-sized bowl, whisk together the flour, baking powder and salt. Set aside.

In a large bowl, use an electric hand mixer to cream together the granulated sugar, butter and vegetable oil for a few minutes, or until pale and creamy. Add the egg, sour cream and lemon zest, and mix on medium speed until well combined. Add half of the flour mixture to the batter and mix on low speed until incorporated. Slowly pour in the lemon juice and milk while mixing on low speed. Add the remaining flour mixture and mix until smooth. Fold the blueberries into the batter.

Portion the cupcake batter into the cupcake liners about three-quarters full. Bake the cupcakes for 20 minutes, or until their tops bounce back when gently touched. Remove them from the oven and let the cupcakes cool in the pan for 5 minutes, then transfer to a wire rack to cool completely.

LEMON CREAM CHEESE FROSTING
In the bowl of a stand mixer fitted with a whisk attachment, whip the butter and cream cheese on medium-high speed until smooth. Add the powdered sugar, lemon zest and salt. While mixing on low speed, drizzle in the lemon juice. Scrape the sides and bottom of the bowl as needed. Turn the mixer to medium-high speed and whip the frosting for an additional 2 to 3 minutes, or until smooth and creamy.

ASSEMBLING THE CUPCAKES
Fill a piping bag fitted with an Ateco 826 piping tip with the lemon cream cheese frosting. Pipe an "ice cream swirl" (see page 15 for more instructions) of frosting onto the cupcakes. Decorate the cupcakes with blueberries and lemon rind curls.

DON'T NEED NOTHIN' BUT NEAPOLITAN CUPCAKES

Don't need nothin' but a Neapolitan cupcake. How can I resist? If you can't decide between vanilla, chocolate and strawberry, get a break from that same old, same old and have all three flavors at once. It don't get better than this! They are made with vanilla and chocolate cake, swirled with strawberry buttercream frosting and topped with Stroopwafels, chocolate sprinkles and cherries. Bring them to the drive-in in the old man's Ford and you will be screaming for more.

VANILLA/CHOCOLATE CUPCAKES

1¼ cups (156 g) all-purpose flour

1½ tsp (7 g) baking powder

½ tsp salt

¾ cup (150 g) granulated sugar

¼ cup (57 g/½ stick) unsalted butter, at room temperature

¼ cup (60 ml) vegetable oil

1 large egg, at room temperature

2 tbsp (30 ml) sour cream, at room temperature

2 tsp (10 ml) vanilla extract

½ cup (120 ml) milk, at room temperature

2 tbsp (12 g) dark cocoa powder

3 tbsp (45 ml) hot water

STRAWBERRY BUTTERCREAM FROSTING

1 cup (227 g/2 sticks) unsalted butter, at room temperature

2½ cups (300 g) powdered sugar

¼ cup (60 ml) strawberry Berrylicious Berry Reduction (page 151)

1 tsp vanilla extract

¼ tsp salt

1 tbsp (15 ml) heavy cream

ADDITIONAL INGREDIENTS

12 Stroopwafel pieces

12 maraschino cherries

1 tbsp (15 g) chocolate sprinkles

VANILLA/CHOCOLATE CUPCAKES

Preheat the oven to 350°F (177°C). Line a cupcake pan with 12 cupcake liners.

In a medium-sized bowl, whisk together the flour, baking powder and salt. Set aside.

In a large bowl, cream together the granulated sugar, butter and vegetable oil with an electric mixer until light and creamy. Add the egg, sour cream and vanilla, and mix on medium speed until smooth. Add half of the flour mixture to the batter and mix on low speed until mostly incorporated. Slowly pour in the milk, continuing to mix on low speed. Add the remaining flour mixture and mix until combined and smooth.

In a small bowl, mix together the dark cocoa powder and water. Divide the cupcake batter in half and add the chocolate mixture to one portion of the batter. Mix well to combine.

Portion the vanilla cupcake batter into the cupcake liners and then add the chocolate cupcake batter on top, filling the liners about three-quarters full. Bake the cupcakes for about 20 minutes, or until the tops of the cupcakes spring back when touched. Remove them from the oven and let the cupcakes cool in the pan for 5 minutes, then transfer to a wire rack to cool completely.

STRAWBERRY BUTTERCREAM FROSTING

In the bowl of a stand mixer fitted with a paddle attachment, whip the butter on medium-high speed for 5 minutes, or until pale and creamy. Add the powdered sugar and mix on low speed until fully incorporated. Add the strawberry reduction, vanilla and salt. Slowly drizzle in the heavy cream. Scrape the sides and bottom of the bowl as needed. Turn the mixer to medium speed and whip the buttercream for 3 to 5 minutes, or until smooth and creamy.

ASSEMBLING THE CUPCAKES

Fill a piping bag fitted with an Ateco 826 piping tip with the strawberry buttercream. Pipe an "ice cream swirl" (see page 15 for more instructions) of frosting onto the cupcakes. Decorate the cupcakes with Stroopwafel pieces, maraschino cherries and chocolate sprinkles.

CLASSIC DESSERTS
Turned Up to 11

You can never go wrong with the classics. Some things withstand the test of time because they are just so darn good. You know, like scrunchies and oversized blazers. Classic desserts have been made time after time and don't disappoint. So, in this chapter, let's transform classic dessert favorites into cupcakes because everything is more fun in cupcake form.

Let's use our handy-dandy shrink ray to miniaturize Black Forest cake and hummingbird cake into scrumptious, handheld treats (pages 132 and 139). Sophisticated tiramisu and elegant crème brûlée will be cupcakified (pages 123 and 127). She may be your cherry pie, but here we are taking Key lime, lemon meringue and Boston cream pies and making them into a sweet surprise (pages 135, 136 and 124) that tastes so good it'll make you cry.

I have only three rules for the cupcakes in this chapter. Number one, avoid bright light. These cupcakes don't do well in the sun and heat. Number two, don't get them wet. The frosting will melt and the cake will be soggy. Number three, don't eat them past midnight. Trust me, you don't want to see what happens. That will take you right into the danger zone. But then again, you just might want to risk it and eat as many as you wish.

TOTAL ECLIPSE OF THE TIRAMISU CUPCAKES

Josie may be on a vacation far away, but these tiramisu cupcakes will have her coming around to talk it over. There are so many things that I wanna say about them, but the taste speaks for itself. To recreate the flavor and texture of the ladyfingers, we are starting off with a light, white almond cake soaked with espresso. The cakes are then swirled with mascarpone whipped cream frosting, dusted with cocoa powder and crowned with a chocolate-covered espresso bean for a little pop of coffee flavor. These cupcakes will make you feel all the love in the world.

WHITE ALMOND CUPCAKES

1¼ cups (156 g) all-purpose flour

1½ tsp (7 g) baking powder

½ tsp salt

¾ cup (150 g) granulated sugar

¼ cup (57 g/½ stick) unsalted butter, at room temperature

¼ cup (60 ml) vegetable oil

2 large egg whites, at room temperature

2 tbsp (30 ml) sour cream, at room temperature

1½ tsp (8 ml) almond extract

1 tsp vanilla extract

½ cup (120 ml) milk, at room temperature

MASCARPONE WHIPPED CREAM FROSTING

8 oz (226 g) mascarpone cheese

½ cup (60 g) powdered sugar

2 tsp (10 ml) vanilla extract

1½ cups (300 ml) heavy cream

ADDITIONAL INGREDIENTS

½ cup (120 ml) brewed espresso, at room temperature

1 tbsp (5 g) unsweetened cocoa powder

12 chocolate-covered espresso beans

WHITE ALMOND CUPCAKES

Preheat the oven to 350°F (177°C). Prepare a cupcake pan with 12 cupcake liners.

In a medium-sized bowl, whisk together the flour, baking powder and salt. Set aside.

In a large bowl, cream together the granulated sugar, butter and vegetable oil with an electric hand mixer until smooth. Add the egg whites, sour cream, almond extract and vanilla, and mix well. Add half of the flour mixture to the batter and mix on low speed until mostly combined. Slowly pour in the milk while mixing on low speed. Add the remaining flour mixture and mix until the batter is smooth.

Portion the cupcake batter into the cupcake liners about three-quarters full. Bake the cupcakes for 20 minutes, or until their tops bounce back when gently touched. Remove them from the oven and let the cupcakes cool in the pan for 5 minutes, then transfer to a wire rack to cool to room temperature.

MASCARPONE WHIPPED CREAM FROSTING

In the bowl of a stand mixer fitted with a whisk attachment, whip the mascarpone cheese, powdered sugar and vanilla until smooth and creamy. On low speed, slowly drizzle in the heavy cream. Scrape the sides and bottom of the bowl. Turn the mixer to medium-high speed and whip until the whipped cream is thick and fluffy.

ASSEMBLING THE CUPCAKES

Poke the tops of the cooled cupcakes a few times with a fork. Slowly spoon the espresso over the cupcakes and allow the espresso to soak in. Fill a piping bag fitted with an Ateco 857 piping tip with the mascarpone whipped cream. Pipe an "ice cream swirl" (see page 15 for more instructions) of frosting onto the cupcakes. Sprinkle the cupcakes with cocoa powder and add a chocolate-covered espresso bean to each cupcake.

BUELLER, BUELLER BOSTON CREAM PIE CUPCAKES

SONG: Journey—Any Way You Want It (1980)

YIELD: 12 cupcakes

She loves to laugh, she loves to sing, she does everything, including baking cupcakes. You'll want to eat these perfectly portioned cupcakes all night, all night, oh every night. Boston cream pie–inspired, they are made with a buttery, yellow cake base filled with creamy vanilla pastry cream filling. To add the taste of bittersweet, the cupcakes are iced with a chocolate ganache frosting and topped with a bit of whipped cream and a maraschino cherry. You won't want to go your separate ways with these little delights, because they will be forever yours, faithfully.

YELLOW CUPCAKES

1¼ cups (156 g) all-purpose flour

1½ tsp (7 g) baking powder

½ tsp salt

¾ cup (150 g) granulated sugar

¼ cup (57 g/½ stick) unsalted butter, at room temperature

¼ cup (60 ml) vegetable oil

1 large egg, at room temperature

2 large egg yolks, at room temperature

1 tbsp (15 ml) sour cream, at room temperature

2 tsp (10 ml) vanilla extract

½ cup (120 ml) milk, at room temperature

WHIPPED CREAM

¾ cup (175 ml) heavy cream

2 tbsp (14 g) powdered sugar

1 tsp vanilla extract

ADDITIONAL INGREDIENTS

1 batch Vanilla Pastry Cream's All I Ever Wanted (page 147)

1 batch Most Excellent Chocolate Ganache Frosting (page 143)

12 maraschino cherries

YELLOW CUPCAKES

Preheat the oven to 350°F (177°C). Prepare a cupcake pan with 12 cupcake liners.

In a medium-sized bowl, whisk together the flour, baking powder and salt. Set aside.

In a large bowl, cream together the granulated sugar, butter and vegetable oil with an electric hand mixer until creamy. Add the egg, egg yolks, sour cream and vanilla, and mix on medium speed until smooth. Add half of the flour mixture and mix on low speed until mostly combined. Slowly pour in the milk while mixing on low speed. Add the remaining flour mixture and mix until the batter is smooth.

Portion the cupcake batter into the cupcake liners about three-quarters full. Bake the cupcakes for 20 minutes, or until their tops spring back when gently touched. Remove them from the oven and let the cupcakes cool in the pan for 5 minutes, then transfer to a wire rack to cool to room temperature.

WHIPPED CREAM

In the bowl of a stand mixer fitted with a whisk attachment, combine the heavy cream, powdered sugar and vanilla, and whip on medium-high speed until medium-stiff peaks form.

ASSEMBLING THE CUPCAKES

Core the cupcakes to remove the center. Use a piping bag with the tip cut off to fill the cupcakes with the vanilla pastry cream. Fill a piping bag fitted with a Wilton 1A piping tip with the chocolate ganache frosting and pipe a "rose swirl" (see page 13 for more instructions) onto the cupcakes. If desired, spread the chocolate ganache with an offset spatula. Fill a piping bag fitted with a Wilton 1M tip with the whipped cream and pipe a small swirl of whipped cream onto the cupcakes. Add a maraschino cherry to each cupcake.

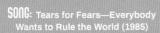

CAUGHT UP IN CRÈME BRÛLÉE CUPCAKES

These cupcakes will send you head over heels. You'll be lost in admiration over this decadent dessert. They are made with fluffy vanilla bean cake and iced with smooth and creamy vanilla pastry cream as the luscious, velvety custard in crème brûlée. To keep the exquisite energy, we are creating a caramelized sugar crust over the pastry cream for that classic crème brûlée taste and elegant appearance. A touch of whipped cream and a raspberry add the perfect touch. Nothing ever lasts forever and these cupcakes certainly will not.

VANILLA BEAN CUPCAKES

1¼ cups (156 g) all-purpose flour

1½ tsp (7 g) baking powder

½ tsp salt

¾ cup (150 g) granulated sugar

¼ cup (57 g/½ stick) unsalted butter, at room temperature

¼ cup (60 ml) vegetable oil

1 large egg, at room temperature

2 tbsp (30 ml) sour cream, at room temperature

2 tsp (10 ml) vanilla extract

1 tsp vanilla bean paste

½ cup (120 ml) milk, at room temperature

WHIPPED CREAM

½ cup (120 ml) heavy cream

1 tbsp (7 g) powdered sugar

½ tsp vanilla extract

ADDITIONAL INGREDIENTS

2 batches Vanilla Pastry Cream's All I Ever Wanted (page 147)

¼ cup (50 g) granulated sugar

12 fresh raspberries

VANILLA BEAN CUPCAKES

Preheat the oven to 350°F (177°C). Line a cupcake pan with 12 cupcake liners.

In a medium-sized bowl, whisk together the flour, baking powder and salt. Set aside.

In a large bowl, use an electric hand mixer on medium speed to cream together the granulated sugar, butter and vegetable oil until pale and creamy. Add the egg, sour cream, vanilla and vanilla bean paste. Mix on medium speed until smooth. Add half of the flour mixture to the batter and mix on low speed until mostly combined. Slowly pour in the milk, continuing to mix on low speed. Add the remaining flour mixture and mix until the batter is smooth.

Portion the cupcake batter into the cupcake liners about three-quarters full. Bake the cupcakes for 20 minutes, or until their tops bounce back when gently touched. Remove them from the oven and let the cupcakes cool in the pan for 5 minutes, then transfer to a wire rack to cool completely.

WHIPPED CREAM

In the bowl of a stand mixer fitted with a whisk attachment, combine the heavy cream, powdered sugar and vanilla. Whip the cream on medium-high speed until medium-stiff peaks form.

ASSEMBLING THE CUPCAKES

Fill a piping bag fitted with a Wilton 1A piping tip with the vanilla pastry cream. Pipe a generous "rose swirl" (see page 13 for more instructions) of pastry cream onto the cupcakes and spread evenly with an offset spatula. Chill the cupcakes for at least 1 hour. Immediately before serving, sprinkle the top of the pastry cream with granulated sugar. Carefully and quickly use a kitchen torch to caramelize the granulated sugar. Fill a piping bag fitted with a Wilton 1M piping tip with the whipped cream. Pipe a small swirl of whipped cream on top of the cupcakes and add fresh raspberries. If you don't have a kitchen torch, you can skip the caramelized sugar and the cupcake will still taste amazing.

BAD (IN A GOOD WAY) BANANA PUDDING CUPCAKES

SONG: Duran Duran—Hungry Like the Wolf (1982)

YIELD: 12 to 14 cupcakes

If you're hungry like the wolf, I implore you to try out this recipe inspired by a southern classic. You'll be on the hunt and after these cupcakes. They are made with a tender banana cake that is filled with rich and creamy vanilla pastry cream, and then iced with cream cheese whipped cream frosting and topped with banana slices and vanilla wafers. Your taste buds will be alive with all the banana goodness because this recipe is a true showstopper.

BANANA CUPCAKES

1¼ cups (156 g) all-purpose flour

1½ tsp (7 g) baking powder

½ tsp salt

¾ cup (150 g) granulated sugar

¼ cup (57 g/½ stick) unsalted butter, at room temperature

¼ cup (60 ml) vegetable oil

⅔ cup (180 g) mashed ripe banana

2 tbsp (30 ml) sour cream, at room temperature

1 large egg, at room temperature

2 tsp (10 ml) vanilla extract

⅓ cup (80 ml) milk, at room temperature

CREAM CHEESE WHIPPED CREAM FROSTING

4 oz (113 g) cream cheese, cold, cubed

½ cup (60 g) powdered sugar

2 tsp (10 ml) vanilla extract

1½ cups (360 ml) heavy cream

ADDITIONAL INGREDIENTS

1 batch Vanilla Pastry Cream's All I Ever Wanted (page 147)

12 to 14 vanilla wafer cookies, plus 2 more to make vanilla wafer crumbs

12 to 14 banana slices

BANANA CUPCAKES

Preheat the oven to 350°F (177°C). Line two cupcake pans with 12 to 14 cupcake liners.

In a medium-sized bowl, whisk together the flour, baking powder and salt. Set aside.

In a large bowl, use an electric hand mixer to cream together the granulated sugar, butter and vegetable oil until creamy. Add the mashed banana, sour cream, egg and vanilla, and mix well. Add half of the flour mixture to the batter and mix on low speed until incorporated. Slowly pour in the milk while mixing on low speed. Add the remaining flour mixture and mix until the batter is smooth.

Portion the cupcake batter into the cupcake liners about three-quarters full. Bake the cupcakes for 20 minutes, or until their tops bounce back when gently touched. Remove them them from the oven and let the cupcakes cool in the pans for 5 minutes, then transfer to a wire rack to cool completely.

CREAM CHEESE WHIPPED CREAM FROSTING

In the bowl of a stand mixer fitted with a whisk attachment, whip the cream cheese, powdered sugar and vanilla for a few minutes until smooth. Turn the mixer to medium speed and slowly drizzle in the heavy cream. Scrape the sides and bottom of the bowl. Turn the mixer to medium-high speed and whip until the whipped cream becomes thick and fluffy.

ASSEMBLING THE CUPCAKES

Core the cupcakes to remove the center. Use a piping bag with the tip cut off to fill the cupcakes with the vanilla pastry cream. Fill a piping bag fitted with an Ateco 826 piping tip with the cream cheese whipped cream frosting. Pipe an "ice cream swirl" (see page 15 for more instructions) of whipped cream onto the cupcakes, then decorate with vanilla wafers, vanilla wafer crumbs and fresh banana slices.

STRAWBERRYLAND STRAWBERRY SHORTCAKE CUPCAKES

These cupcakes will put the boom-boom into your heart and send your soul sky high. If there is a dessert that will make you do the jitterbug, strawberry shortcake is it. They are made with fluffy angel food cake frosted with cream cheese whipped cream frosting. Fresh strawberries transform these angelic cupcakes from a careless whisper to the edge of heaven. Wake me up before you make these cupcakes, because I was dreaming, but I should have been baking instead.

ANGEL FOOD CUPCAKES

¾ cup (150 g) granulated sugar

½ cup (60 g) cake flour

¼ tsp salt

5 large egg whites, at room temperature

1 tbsp (15 ml) warm water

¾ tsp cream of tartar

½ tsp vanilla extract

½ tsp almond extract

CREAM CHEESE WHIPPED CREAM FROSTING

4 oz (113 g) cream cheese, cold

½ cup (60 g) powdered sugar

2 tsp (10 ml) vanilla extract

1½ cups (355 ml) heavy cream

ADDITIONAL INGREDIENTS

1 cup (160 g) finely chopped fresh strawberries

ANGEL FOOD CUPCAKES

Preheat the oven to 325°F (162°C). Line a cupcake pan with 12 cupcake liners.

Pulse the granulated sugar in a food processor until very fine. Divide the sugar in half. In a large mixing bowl, sift together one portion of the granulated sugar with the cake flour and salt. Set aside.

In the bowl of a stand mixer fitted with a whisk attachment, combine the egg whites, warm water, cream of tartar, vanilla and almond extract. Mix on low speed until frothy. Turn the speed to medium and slowly sprinkle in the other portion of the granulated sugar. Increase the mixer speed to medium-high and whip the egg whites until soft peaks form.

Pour the flour mixture into the egg whites and gently fold until the batter is smooth. Do not overmix the cupcake batter.

Portion the cupcake batter into the cupcake liners, filling the liners to the very top. Bake the cupcakes for 22 to 24 minutes, or until their tops bounce back when gently touched. Remove them from the oven and let the cupcakes cool in the pan for 5 minutes, then transfer to a wire rack to cool completely.

CREAM CHEESE WHIPPED CREAM FROSTING

In the bowl of a stand mixer fitted with a whisk attachment, whip the cream cheese, powdered sugar and vanilla until smooth and creamy. On low speed, slowly drizzle in the heavy cream. Turn the mixer to medium-high speed and whip until the whipped cream is light and fluffy.

ASSEMBLING THE CUPCAKES

Fill a piping bag fitted with an Ateco 826 piping tip with the cream cheese whipped cream frosting. Pipe a "double swirl" (see page 13 for more instructions) of the whipped cream onto the cupcakes, leaving the center of the cupcake open to create a bit of a well. Add the chopped fresh strawberries in the center of the whipped cream.

BLACK TO THE FOREST CUPCAKES

SONG: Prince—Let's Go Crazy (1984)

YIELD: 14 cupcakes

Dearly beloved, we have gathered here today to bake through this thing called life. If you are feeling a bit too leisurely, pull out this recipe. These cupcakes are heavenly chocolate cake filled with homemade cherry filling and topped with fluffy vanilla whipped cream frosting. You better love 'em and eat 'em fast, because these cupcakes simply won't last. So, let's go crazy and eat the whole batch because you better live now before the grim reaper comes knocking on your door.

CHOCOLATE CUPCAKES

1 cup (125 g) all-purpose flour

1 cup (200 g) granulated sugar

⅓ cup (33 g) dark cocoa powder

1 tsp baking soda

½ tsp baking powder

½ tsp salt

½ cup (120 ml) milk, at room temperature

¼ cup (60 ml) vegetable oil

1 large egg, at room temperature

1 tsp vanilla extract

½ cup (120 ml) boiling water

WHIPPED CREAM FROSTING

2 cups (475 ml) heavy cream

½ cup (60 g) powdered sugar

1 tsp vanilla extract

ADDITIONAL INGREDIENTS

1 batch cherry Funky Fresh Fruit Filling (page 148)

1 tbsp (15 g) chocolate sprinkles

14 fresh or maraschino cherries

CHOCOLATE CUPCAKES

Preheat the oven to 350°F (177°C). Prepare two cupcake pans with 14 cupcake liners.

In a large bowl, whisk together the flour, granulated sugar, dark cocoa powder, baking soda, baking powder and salt. Add the milk, vegetable oil, egg and vanilla, and whisk until well combined. Pour in the boiling water and whisk until the batter is smooth.

Pour the cupcake batter into the cupcake liners about two-thirds full. Bake the cupcakes for 20 to 22 minutes, or until their tops spring back when gently touched. Remove them from the oven and let the cupcakes cool in the pans for 5 minutes, then transfer to a wire rack to cool completely.

WHIPPED CREAM FROSTING

In the bowl of a stand mixer fitted with a whisk attachment, mix together the heavy cream, powdered sugar and vanilla on low speed until frothy. Turn the mixer to medium-high speed and whip until medium-stiff peaks form.

ASSEMBLING THE CUPCAKES

Core the cupcakes to remove the center. Use a piping bag with the tip cut off to fill the cupcakes with the cherry filling. Fill a piping bag fitted with an Ateco 826 piping tip with the whipped cream frosting. Pipe an "ice cream swirl" (see page 15 for more instructions) of frosting onto the cupcakes. Decorate the cupcakes with chocolate sprinkles and cherries.

KEEP ON LOVIN' KEY LIME PIE CUPCAKES

You won't have to think twice before diving into these cupcakes. Your lips will have a sweet surprise when they taste these tart and tempting treats. They are made with fluffy Key lime cake with a kick of Key lime zest and juice to whet your appetite. A swirl of creamy Key lime buttercream frosting, graham cracker crumbs and a slice of Key lime will make you blush. You will keep on lovin' these Key lime cupcakes because they will tease you and unease you, all the better just to please you.

KEY LIME CUPCAKES

1¼ cups (156 g) all-purpose flour

1½ tsp (7 g) baking powder

½ tsp salt

¾ cup (150 g) granulated sugar

¼ cup (57 g/½ stick) unsalted butter, at room temperature

¼ cup (60 ml) vegetable oil

1 large egg, at room temperature

2 tbsp (30 ml) sour cream, at room temperature

1 tsp Key lime zest

¼ cup (60 ml) fresh Key lime juice

¼ cup (60 ml) milk, at room temperature

KEY LIME BUTTERCREAM FROSTING

1 cup (227 g/2 sticks) unsalted butter, at room temperature

14 oz (396 g) sweetened condensed milk

1 tsp Key lime zest

¼ tsp salt

¼ cup (60 ml) fresh Key lime juice

ADDITIONAL INGREDIENTS

¼ cup (30 g) graham cracker crumbs

12 Key lime slices

KEY LIME CUPCAKES

Preheat the oven to 350°F (177°C). Line a cupcake pan with 12 cupcake liners.

In a medium-sized bowl, whisk together the flour, baking powder and salt. Set aside.

In a large bowl, use an electric hand mixer to cream the granulated sugar, butter and vegetable oil until creamy. Add the egg, sour cream and Key lime zest and mix on medium speed until well combined. Add half of the flour mixture to the batter and mix on low speed until incorporated. Slowly pour in the Key lime juice and milk while mixing on low speed. Add the remaining flour mixture and mix until the batter is smooth.

Portion the cupcake batter into the cupcake liners about three-quarters full. Bake the cupcakes for 20 minutes, or until their tops bounce back when gently touched. Remove them from the oven and let the cupcakes cool in the pan for 5 minutes, then transfer to a wire rack to cool completely.

KEY LIME BUTTERCREAM FROSTING

In the bowl of a stand mixer fitted with the whisk attachment, whip the softened butter for 5 minutes, or until pale and creamy. While mixing on medium speed, slowly pour in the sweetened condensed milk, add the Key lime zest and salt, and drizzle in the Key lime juice. Scrape the sides and bottom of the bowl. Whip the buttercream for 5 to 10 minutes, or until it thickens up and becomes creamy and smooth.

ASSEMBLING THE CUPCAKES

Fill a piping bag fitted with a Wilton 1A piping tip with the Key lime frosting. Pipe an "ice cream swirl" (see page 15 for more instructions) of frosting onto the cupcakes. Decorate the cupcakes with graham cracker crumbs and Key lime slices.

NOTE: You can replace the Key lime zest, juice and slices with regular lime.

LUCKY STAR LEMON MERINGUE PIE CUPCAKES

SONG: Starship—Nothing's Gonna Stop Us Now (1987)

YIELD: 12 cupcakes

Why build the perfect mannequin when you can bake the perfect cupcake? Although these won't be coming to life in a department store window, they will certainly thrill your taste buds. Nothing's gonna stop us from baking up a batch of these sweet and tart cupcakes, made with a fluffy lemon cake, filled with tart lemon curd and iced with a creamy, luscious toasted meringue frosting.

LEMON CUPCAKES

1¼ cups (156 g) all-purpose flour
1½ tsp (7 g) baking powder
½ tsp salt
¾ cup (150 g) granulated sugar
¼ cup (57 g/½ stick) unsalted butter, at room temperature
¼ cup (60 ml) vegetable oil
1 large egg, at room temperature
2 tbsp (30 ml) sour cream, at room temperature
1 tsp lemon zest
¼ cup (60 ml) fresh lemon juice
¼ cup (60 ml) milk, at room temperature

MERINGUE FROSTING

4 large egg whites
¾ cup (150 g) granulated sugar
¼ tsp cream of tartar
1 tsp vanilla extract

LEMON CURD

3 egg yolks
½ cup (100 g) granulated sugar
¼ cup (60 ml) fresh lemon juice
½ tsp lemon zest
¼ cup (57 g/½ stick) unsalted butter, cold, cubed

LEMON CUPCAKES

Preheat the oven to 350°F (177°C). Line a cupcake pan with 12 cupcake liners.

In a medium-sized bowl, whisk together the flour, baking powder and salt. Set aside.

In a large bowl, cream together the granulated sugar, butter and vegetable oil with an electric mixer until it is pale and creamy. Add the egg, sour cream and lemon zest, and mix on medium speed until well combined. Add half of the flour mixture to the batter and mix on low speed until incorporated. Slowly pour in the lemon juice and milk while mixing on low speed. Add the remaining flour mixture and mix until combined and smooth.

Portion the cupcake batter into the cupcake liners about three-quarters full. Bake the cupcakes for 20 minutes, or until their tops bounce back when gently touched. Remove them from the oven and let the cupcakes cool in the pan for 5 minutes, then transfer to a wire rack to cool completely.

MERINGUE FROSTING

In a heatproof bowl over a pot of simmering water on the stovetop, whisk together the egg whites, granulated sugar and cream of tartar until the sugar granules are dissolved. Transfer the egg white mixture to the bowl of a stand mixer fitted with a whisk attachment. Add the vanilla. Whip the egg whites on medium-high speed until glossy, stiff peaks form.

LEMON CURD

In a medium-sized saucepan, whisk together the egg yolks, granulated sugar and lemon juice over low heat on the stovetop. Cook the mixture, whisking occasionally, for about 10 minutes, or until thickened. Add the lemon zest. Remove the saucepan from the heat and add the cubed butter, one piece at a time, whisking in between each addition. Cool the lemon curd to room temperature and then chill for at least 2 hours.

ASSEMBLING THE CUPCAKES

Core the cupcakes to remove the center and fill with the lemon curd. Fill a piping bag fitted with an Ateco 857 piping tip with the meringue frosting. Pipe an "ice cream swirl" (see page 15 for more instructions) of frosting onto the cupcakes and use a kitchen torch to carefully toast the meringue. If you don't have a kitchen torch, you can skip the toasting and the cupcakes will still be absolutely delicious.

DON'T PUT YOUR HEEL DOWN HUMMINGBIRD CUPCAKES

If you've got hungry eyes for banana, pineapple and pecans, these cupcakes will have you dirty dancing. The incredibly moist and tender cakes are made with banana and pineapple for a bit of a tropical twist. We don't need to carry a watermelon here, just a pineapple. On top, they are swirled and twirled with a tangy cream cheese frosting and sprinkled with chopped pecans. You'll never be sorry for eating one, because the truth is, nobody puts these cupcakes in a corner.

HUMMINGBIRD CUPCAKES

1¼ cups (156 g) all-purpose flour

1½ tsp (7 g) baking powder

1 tsp ground cinnamon

½ tsp salt

¾ cup (150 g) granulated sugar

¼ cup (57 g/½ stick) unsalted butter, at room temperature

¼ cup (60 ml) vegetable oil

1 large egg, at room temperature

2 tbsp (30 ml) sour cream, at room temperature

2 tsp (10 ml) vanilla extract

⅓ cup (85 g) mashed banana

⅓ cup (85 g) undrained, crushed pineapple

2 tbsp (30 ml) pineapple juice

¼ cup (36 g) finely chopped pecans

CREAM CHEESE FROSTING

¾ cup (170 g/1½ sticks) unsalted butter, at room temperature

4 oz (113 g) cream cheese, at room temperature

2½ cups (300 g) powdered sugar

2 tsp (10 ml) vanilla extract

¼ tsp salt

ADDITIONAL INGREDIENTS

12 or 13 banana chips

½ cup (80 g) dried pineapple pieces

¼ cup (36 g) finely chopped pecans

HUMMINGBIRD CUPCAKES

Preheat the oven to 350°F (177°C). Line two cupcake pans with 12 or 13 cupcake liners.

In a medium-sized bowl, whisk together the flour, baking powder, cinnamon and salt. Set aside.

In a large bowl, use an electric hand mixer to cream the granulated sugar, butter and vegetable oil until pale and creamy. Add the egg, sour cream and vanilla, and mix well. Add the mashed banana and crushed pineapple, and mix to incorporate. Add half of the flour mixture to the batter and mix on low speed. Slowly pour in the pineapple juice while mixing on low speed. Add the remaining flour mixture and mix until the batter is smooth. Fold in the chopped pecans.

Portion the cupcake batter into the cupcake liners about three-quarters full. Bake the cupcakes for 20 minutes, or until their tops bounce back when gently touched. Remove them from the oven and let the cupcakes cool in the pans for 5 minutes, then transfer to a wire rack to cool completely.

CREAM CHEESE FROSTING

In the bowl of a stand mixer fitted with a whisk attachment, whip the butter and cream cheese on medium-high speed until smooth. Add the powdered sugar, vanilla and salt. Mix on low speed until combined. Scrape the sides and bottom of the bowl as needed. Turn the mixer to medium-high speed and whip the frosting for an additional 2 to 3 minutes, or until smooth and creamy.

ASSEMBLING THE CUPCAKES

Fill a piping bag fitted with an Ateco 857 piping tip with the cream cheese frosting. Pipe an "ice cream swirl" (see page 15 for more instructions) of frosting onto the cupcakes. Decorate the cupcakes with banana chips, dried pineapple and finely chopped pecans.

SWEET DREAMS ARE
Made of These

Welcome to the chapter of all things extra. This is where we add fun, flavor and flair to the cupcakes. Many of the cupcake and frosting recipes in this book rely on a little something extra to bump things up to the next level, and here you will find it all. As we all know from '80s fashion, it is important to accessorize. So, think of this chapter as the leg warmers to your spandex, the rhinestone glove to your red leather jacket and the banana clip to your overly teased hair.

In this chapter, I will share with you a super simple chocolate ganache (page 143), salted caramel sauce (page 144), smooth and creamy vanilla pastry cream (page 147) and fantastically versatile fruit filling (page 148). I will also teach you how to make the secret ingredient in all my berry cupcakes and buttercreams that provides a blast of berry flavor (page 151). Once you master these components, you will be drizzling, filling and frosting like a pro.

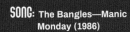

SONG: The Bangles—Manic Monday (1986)

YIELD DRIZZLE: ¼ cup (60 ml)

YIELD FROSTING: 1 cup (236 ml) to frost 12 cupcakes

MOST EXCELLENT CHOCOLATE GANACHE

Earth girls may be easy, but not as easy as this two-ingredient chocolate ganache recipe. Chocolate ganache can be used as a drizzle over the Milk's Favorite Cookie Cupcakes (page 64) or used as frosting on Bueller, Bueller Boston Cream Pie Cupcakes (page 124). To make things extra easy, we are going to be making it in a microwave. In just a minute or two, you will have smooth chocolate ganache that is shinier than your father's 1961 Ferrari 250 GT California Spyder.

CHOCOLATE GANACHE DRIZZLE
¼ cup (42 g) semisweet or dark chocolate chips

2 tbsp (30 ml) heavy cream

CHOCOLATE GANACHE FROSTING
1 cup (168 g) semisweet or dark chocolate chips

½ cup (120 ml) heavy cream

CHOCOLATE GANACHE DRIZZLE
Pour the chocolate chips into a heatproof bowl. In a separate, microwave-safe bowl, heat the cream in a microwave for about 30 seconds, or until bubbling. Pour the hot cream over the chocolate chips and allow the mixture to sit for 2 minutes to melt the chocolate. Stir the mixture until smooth and shiny.

Allow the chocolate ganache to cool slightly before drizzling onto the cupcakes. Use a piping bag or squeeze bottle to add the perfect ganache drizzle.

CHOCOLATE GANACHE FROSTING
Follow the same directions as for the chocolate ganache drizzle. Allow the ganache to cool completely, stirring occasionally, until it has a spreadable consistency like peanut butter. You can speed up the cooling process by chilling the ganache in the refrigerator, stirring every few minutes, until it reaches a spreadable consistency.

CHOCOLATE GANACHE TIPS AND TRICKS

- You can make as much chocolate ganache as you would like. The ratio for a chocolate ganache drizzle is 2 parts chocolate to 1 part heavy cream (example: 1 cup chocolate to ½ cup heavy cream). If you would like to double or triple the recipe, you may need to heat the cream in a microwave for an additional 15 to 30 seconds.

- The chocolate ganache should be slightly warm when drizzling. If the ganache is too hot, it can melt the buttercream frosting.

- Chill the frosted cupcakes in the refrigerator for about 15 minutes before drizzling the warm ganache onto the frosting to ensure the buttercream holds its shape and does not melt.

- Store any leftover chocolate ganache in an airtight container in the refrigerator for up to 2 weeks.

STICKY SWEET SALTED CARAMEL SAUCE

SONG: Eurythmics—Sweet Dreams Are Made of This (1983)

YIELD: ¾ cup (177 ml)

Sweet dreams are made of salted caramel sauce. Who am I to disagree? This salted caramel sauce can be found in several of my cupcake recipes as a filling, a component in salted caramel buttercream frosting and also to drizzle over the top of the cupcakes. Making caramel sauce from scratch can feel overwhelming, but this simple recipe will have you holding your head up and doing it over and over again. So, pour some sugar into your saucepan, and let's make some homemade salted caramel sauce.

1 cup (200 g) granulated sugar

¼ cup (57 g/½ stick) unsalted butter, cubed, at room temperature

¼ cup (60 ml) heavy cream, at room temperature

1 tsp vanilla extract

½ tsp salt

Pour the granulated sugar into a medium-sized saucepan and place over low heat on the stovetop. Use a wooden spoon to constantly stir the sugar and break up any sugar clumps that form as the sugar begins to melt. Continue to stir until all the sugar is melted and turns light golden-brown. Immediately remove the saucepan from the heat to prevent the caramel from burning.

Add the cubed butter one piece at a time, mixing well in between each addition, being careful to avoid the steam. Once the butter is melted, pour in the heavy cream and stir until fully incorporated and smooth. The caramel will bubble up. Add the vanilla and salt, and mix until well combined. If you notice any lumps, run the caramel through a fine-mesh sieve. Pour the salted caramel sauce into a heatproof container and let it cool to room temperature before using.

Make the salted caramel sauce ahead and store in the refrigerator for up to 2 weeks. To use, heat the caramel sauce in a microwave in 15-second intervals, stirring in between each interval, until the caramel loosens up and has a drizzle consistency.

SONG: Lionel Richie—All Night Long (1983)

YIELD: 1 cup (236 ml) to fill approximately 12 cupcakes

VANILLA PASTRY CREAM'S ALL I EVER WANTED

Well, my friends, the time has come to share my recipe for vanilla pastry cream. Pastry cream is a rich, thick custard that can be used to fill desserts such as cream puffs, éclairs and, yes, even cupcakes. This pastry cream is flavored with vanilla bean paste for an amazing vanilla flavor. Life is good, wild and sweet when you are filling cupcakes with vanilla pastry cream.

½ cup (120 ml) heavy cream

½ cup (120 ml) whole milk, divided

3 tbsp (45 g) granulated sugar

1½ tbsp (12 g) cornstarch

1 large egg yolk

1 tbsp (14 g) unsalted butter, cold, cubed

1 tsp vanilla bean paste

In a small saucepan, combine the heavy cream and ¼ cup (60 ml) of the milk. Place the saucepan over medium-low heat to scald the cream.

While the cream mixture is heating, in a medium-sized bowl, whisk together the granulated sugar, cornstarch, egg yolk and remaining ¼ cup (60 ml) of milk until smooth. Slowly drizzle in the hot cream mixture while whisking, to temper the egg mixture. Transfer the custard back to the small saucepan and cook over medium-low heat, whisking constantly, until thickened.

Remove the saucepan from the heat and whisk in the cubed butter and vanilla bean paste. Run the custard through a fine-mesh sieve to remove any lumps. Let the pastry cream cool to room temperature and then cover and chill in the refrigerator for at least 2 hours. Stir well before using as cupcake filling.

Make the vanilla pastry cream ahead and store in the refrigerator for up to 1 week.

FUNKY FRESH FRUIT FILLING

SONG: Prince—Raspberry Beret (1985)

YIELD: 1 cup (236 ml) to fill approximately 12 cupcakes

Believe it or not, homemade fruit filling is incredibly easy to make and tastes so much better than store-bought. With just a handful of ingredients and a few minutes, you will have a delicious cupcake filling that is bursting with fruit flavor. This fruit filling is used in several recipes in this book, including It's Peanut Butter Jelly Time Cupcakes (page 49) and Black to the Forest Cupcakes (page 132). So, put on your raspberry beret and let's whip up some sweet fruit cupcake filling.

8 oz (227 g) frozen raspberries, strawberries or cherries

2 tbsp (30 g) granulated sugar

2 tsp (10 ml) fresh lemon juice

1 tbsp (8 g) cornstarch

1 tbsp (15 ml) room temperature water

In a small saucepan, combine the frozen fruit, granulated sugar and lemon juice. Cook the fruit over medium-low heat, stirring occasionally, until the fruit has broken down and the mixture is bubbling. Break up the berries or cherries with a spoon as they soften.

In a small bowl, stir together the cornstarch and water to create a slurry. Slowly drizzle the cornstarch slurry into the fruit filling while vigorously stirring, until the fruit filling thickens.

Transfer the filling to a heatproof bowl and let it cool to room temperature. If you are making raspberry filling, I recommend running the filling through a fine-mesh sieve, pushing the raspberry filling through the sieve with a spoon to remove the seeds. Chill the fruit filling for 2 hours before use.

Make the fruit filling ahead and store in the refrigerator for up to 1 week.

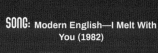

BERRYLICIOUS BERRY REDUCTION

Berry reduction is a component in several of the cupcake and buttercream frosting recipes in this book. The only ingredient you will need to make it is frozen berries. I love using berry reduction in my recipes because it adds amazing, fresh berry flavor and tastes so much better than artificial extracts. You'll see the difference and it's getting better all the time.

16 oz (454 g) frozen berries (raspberries, strawberries, blackberries or triple berry blend)

Place the frozen berries in a saucepan, then cook them over medium-low heat, stirring occasionally, for 10 to 15 minutes, or until the berries are soft and the liquid has reduced slightly.

Remove the saucepan from the heat and allow the berry mixture to cool. Use an immersion blender or a food processor to create a smooth purée. Run the purée through a fine-mesh sieve to remove the seeds. Transfer the berry reduction to a storage container.

Make the berry reduction ahead of time and store in the refrigerator for 1 week. Bring the berry reduction to room temperature before adding it to cupcake batter or buttercream frosting.

GIRLS JUST WANNA BAKE CUPCAKES
MIXTAPE SONG INDEX

- **a-ha—Take On Me**—*Take On These Caramel Corn Cupcakes*
- **The B-52's— Love Shack**—*Bang Bang Bang Blackberry Peach Cupcakes*
- **Bananarama—Cruel Summer**—*Bananarama Split Cupcakes*
- **The Bangles—Manic Monday**—*Most Excellent Chocolate Ganache*
- **The Beach Boys—Kokomo**—*If You Like Piña Colada Cupcakes*
- **Belinda Carlisle—Heaven Is a Place on Earth**—*Stellar Strawberry Cupcakes*
- **Billy Idol—White Wedding**—*It's a Nice Day for White Wedding Cupcakes*
- **Billy Ocean—Get Outta My Dreams, Get Into My Car**—*Straight Up S'mores Cupcakes*
- **Bon Jovi—Bad Medicine**—*So Satisfying Candy Bar Cupcakes*
- **Bow Wow Wow—I Want Candy**—*Pop Goes the Cupcake*
- **The Cars—You Might Think**—*Hostess with the Mostest Cupcakes*
- **Culture Club—Karma Chameleon**—*Karma Candyland Cupcakes*
- **Cyndi Lauper—Girls Just Want to Have Fun**—*Livin' on Lemon Blueberry Cupcakes*
- **David Bowie—Let's Dance**—*Stardust Circus Animal Cookie Cupcakes*
- **Dead or Alive—You Spin Me Round (Like a Record)**—*Nobody Better Lay a Finger on My Cupcakes*
- **Def Leppard—Pour Some Sugar on Me**—*'80s Movie Night Cupcakes*
- **Duran Duran—Hungry Like the Wolf**—*Bad (in a Good Way) Banana Pudding Cupcakes*
- **Eddie Money—Take Me Home Tonight**—*Centerfold Chocolate Chip Cookie Cupcakes*
- **Eric Carmen—Hungry Eyes**—*Don't Put Your Heel Down Hummingbird Cupcakes*
- **Eurythmics—Sweet Dreams Are Made of This**—*Sticky Sweet Salted Caramel Sauce*

- **Genesis—Invisible Touch**—*Fancy-Schmancy Chocolate Hazelnut Cupcakes*
- **Gloria Estefan—Conga**—*Shake Your Cherry Limeade Cupcakes*
- **Hall and Oates—You Make My Dreams Come True**—*Awesome Ice Cream Cone Cupcakes*
- **Huey Lewis and the News—The Power of Love**—*Valley Girl Vanilla Bean Cupcakes*
- **The Human League—Don't You Want Me**—*Roll a Caramel Candy to Your Cupcakes*
- **Irene Cara—Flashdance...What a Feeling**—*Killer Carrot Cake Cupcakes*
- **Jackson Browne—Somebody's Baby**—*Milk's Favorite Cookie Cupcakes*
- **Journey—Any Way You Want It**—*Bueller, Bueller Boston Cream Pie Cupcakes*
- **Kate Bush—Running Up That Hill**—*L'eggo My Cupcakes*
- **Kenny Loggins—Footloose**—*Lose Your Blues Triple Berry Cupcakes*
- **Kim Carnes—Bette Davis Eyes**—*Keep On Lovin' Key Lime Pie Cupcakes*
- **Kool & The Gang—Celebration**—*Big Time Birthday Cupcakes*
- **Lindsey Buckingham—Holiday Road**—*Rockin' Raspberry Lemonade Cupcakes*
- **Lionel Richie—All Night Long**—*Vanilla Pastry Cream's All I Ever Wanted*
- **Madonna—Holiday**—*Cowabunga Confetti Cupcakes*
- **Michael Jackson—The Way You Make Me Feel**—*Smooth Criminal Snickerdoodle Cupcakes*
- **Modern English—I Melt With You**—*Berrylicious Berry Reduction*
- **Naked Eyes—Always Something There to Remind Me**—*Snap, Crackle, Pop Crispy Rice Treats Cupcakes*
- **Nena—99 Red Balloons**—*Radical Red Velvet Cupcakes*
- **New Kids on the Block—You Got It (The Right Stuff)**—*You've Got the Fluffy Stuff Cupcakes*

- **Orchestral Manoeuvres in the Dark—If You Leave**—*Dreamy Dreamsicle Cupcakes*

- **The Outfield—Your Love**—*Total Eclipse of the Tiramisu Cupcakes*

- **Poison—Nothin' But a Good Time**—*Don't Need Nothin' but Neapolitan Cupcakes*

- **Prince—Let's Go Crazy**—*Black to the Forest Cupcakes*

- **Prince—Raspberry Beret**—*Funky Fresh Fruit Filling*

- **The Psychedelic Furs—Pretty in Pink**—*Pretty in Pink Cherry Cupcakes*

- **Ray Parker Jr.—Ghostbusters**—*Fantabulous Fluffernutter Cupcakes*

- **Real Life—Send Me an Angel**—*It's Peanut Butter Jelly Time Cupcakes*

- **Rick Astley—Never Gonna Give You Up**—*Oatrageous Oatmeal Creme Pie Cupcakes*

- **Robert Palmer—Simply Irresistible**—*Sugar and Spice Cookie Cupcakes*

- **The Romantics—Talking in Your Sleep**—*Mad about Mint Chocolate Cookie Cupcakes*

- **Simple Minds—Don't You (Forget About Me)**—*Breakfast Club Cupcakes*

- **Soft Cell—Tainted Love**—*Legit Lemon Cupcakes*

- **A Flock of Seagulls—Space Age Love Song**—*Space Age Brownie Cupcakes*

- **Spandau Ballet—True**—*Sixteen Candles Sprinkle Cookie Cupcakes*

- **Starship—Nothing's Gonna Stop Us Now**—*Lucky Star Lemon Meringue Pie Cupcakes*

- **Tears for Fears—Everybody Wants to Rule the World**—*Caught Up in Crème Brûlée Cupcakes*

- **Tommy Tutone—867-5309/Jenny**—*Stunning Strawberry Crunch Cupcakes*

- **Wang Chung—Everybody Have Fun Tonight**—*Totally Tubular Chocolate Cupcakes*

- **Wham!—Wake Me Up Before You Go-Go**—*Strawberryland Strawberry Shortcake Cupcakes*

- **Whitney Houston—I Wanna Dance With Somebody**—*Feeling Kinda Nutty Cupcakes*

ACKNOWLEDGMENTS

To the Cake Me Home Tonight community: You are totally rad, awesome, killer, righteous and tubular. This book would not have been possible without your support. Thank you for the likes, follows, comments, shares, views, and of course, for trying out my recipes.

To my husband, Chris: Thank you for always believing in me, supporting my dreams and being the world's best taste tester. You are my everything and I could not have created this book without you. You're my inspiration.

To my daughters, Carmen and Charlie: Thank you for always licking the frosting and leaving the cupcake for me. You are my best girls and I'm sending you all the love in the world.

To my sister and best friend, Gretchen: You are the E.T. to my Elliot. The Ferris to my Cameron. The Goose to my Maverick. Thank you for helping me with '80s references and always keeping me grounded.

To my mother, Sharon: Thank you for being my baking assistant when I unexpectedly broke my leg during the recipe development process. I am forever grateful for your love, support and encouragement.

To my mother-in-law and father-in-law, Tracy and Mike: Thank you for watching the girls so I could bake and decorate hundreds of cupcakes. Your support during this process was invaluable.

To my friends and family: Thank you for always coming hungry and knowing that cupcakes are what is on the menu. Your taste testing skills are unmatched.

To my photo editor/photographer, James: I aspire to be as insanely talented at food photography as you. Thank you for your guidance, collaboration and support, and for making each one of these cupcake photos shine.

To my branding photographer, Mark: Thank you for letting me throw sprinkles around your studio and for capturing stunning images that make me feel strong and beautiful.

To my incredible editors, Krystle and Sarah: Thank you for guiding me through this process, answering my questions, supporting me and cheering me on. Your kindness, assistance and flexibility have truly made this a wonderful and rewarding experience.

To the Page Street Publishing team: Thank you for trusting me and allowing me to share my recipes with the world. I am truly grateful for this life-changing opportunity.

ABOUT THE AUTHOR

Courtney Carey is the recipe developer, blogger and food photographer behind Cake Me Home Tonight, a popular baking blog focused on easy and delicious dessert recipes for home bakers.

Courtney is a self-taught baker who has a serious love for cupcakes and all things '80s. With over 20 years of experience baking and developing recipes, Courtney loves to share simple and irresistible dessert recipes along with baking tips and tutorials to make baking fun and stress-free. Her goal with Cake Me Home Tonight is to inspire new bakers and help home bakers to build baking confidence.

Courtney is a proud Western New Yorker. When she is not in the kitchen, she works as a licensed mental health counselor, and is a wife and mother to two beautiful girls. Courtney loves cooking, camping, boating, musical theater, mixing up fancy cocktails, '80s music and movies, and watching football. (Go, Bills!)

You can find Courtney's recipes on cakemehometonight.com, or follow along on social media for dessert recipes and tons of '80s tunes.

    @cakemehometonight

cakemehometonight.com

INDEX